Simon Armitag

IAN GREGSON was born in Manchester and edi
He has written for the *Los Angeles Times Book Rev*   ___ poems
and reviews in the *London Review of Books*, the *TLS* and *Poetry Review*, amongst
others. His critical books are *Contemporary Poetry and Postmodernism*; *The
Male Image: Representations of Masculinity in Postwar Poetry* (both published by
Macmillan); *Postmodern Literature* (Hodder Arnold, 2004), *Character and Satire in Postwar Fiction* (Continuum, 2006) and *The New Poetry In Wales* (University of Wales Press, 2007). He has lived most of his adult life in North Wales
where he teaches in the English department at the university in Bangor.

Simon Armitage

IAN GREGSON
BANGOR UNIVERSITY

SALT
LONDON

PUBLISHED BY SALT PUBLISHING
Dutch House, 307–308 High Holborn, London WC1V 7LL United Kingdom

The right of Ian Gregson to be identified as the
author of this work has been asserted by him in accordance
with Section 77 of the Copyright, Designs and Patents Act 1988.

First published 2011

Printed and bound in the United Kingdom by Lightning Source UK Ltd
Typeset in Swift 9.5 / 13

ISBN 978 1 84771 767 5 paperback

1 3 5 7 9 8 6 4 2

CONTENTS

ACKNOWLEDGEMENTS

I AM GRATEFUL to Faber and Faber for permission to quote from *The Dead Sea Poems*, *Kid*, *Book of Matches*, *The Universal Home Doctor* and *Seeing Stars*; to Bloodaxe for permission to quote from *Zoom*; to Simon Armitage for permission to quote from *Xanadu*; and to David Godwin Associates for US permissions.

ARMITAGE'S TEXTS

THE BOOKS BY Simon Armitage referred to in this book are (in chronological order):

Zoom! (Bloodaxe: Newcastle Upon Tyne, 1989)

Xanadu (Bloodaxe: Newcastle Upon Tyne, 1992)

Kid (London: Faber, 1992)

Book of Matches (London: Faber, 1993)

The Dead Sea Poems (London: Faber, 1995)

Moon Country: Further Reports from Iceland, with Glyn Maxwell (London: Faber, 1996)

CloudCuckooLand (London: Faber, 1997)

All Points North (Harmondsworth: Penguin, 1998)

Killing Time (London: Faber, 1999)

Little Green Man (London: Penguin, 2001)

The Universal Home Doctor (London: Faber, 2002)

Travelling Songs (London: Faber, 2002)

The White Stuff (London: Penguin, 2005)

Jerusalem (London: Faber, 2005)

Tyrannosaurus Rex Versus the Corduroy Kid (London: Faber, 2007)

Sir Gawain and the Green Knight (London: Faber, 2007)

The Not Dead (Hebden Bridge: Pomona, 2008)

Out of the Blue (London: Enitharmon, 2008)

Gig (London: Penguin, 2008)

The Poetry of Birds, with Tim Dee (London: Penguin, 2009)

Seeing Stars (London: Faber, 2010)

INTRODUCTION

SIMON ARMITAGE IS one of the most compelling figures in contemporary literature, most conspicuously because of his charismatic style:

Sweatshop, mop and bucket,
given brush, shop floor,
slipped up, clocked in
half stoned, shown door.

Backwoodsman number, joiner,
timber, lumber, trouble,
axe fell, sacked for prank
with spirit-level bubble.

Sales rep, basic training,
car, own boss, P.A.
commission, targets,
stuff that, cards same day.

These lines from 'C.V.' (*The Dead Sea Poems*, p. 7) are characteristic in creating a surface that immediately grabs attention with driving rhythms and colloquial energy. They are created in this case by short lines and obvious rhymes, and by the exclusion of definite, and indefinite, articles, and of conjunctions, so that nouns and verbs are made emphatically prominent. The resultant fast pacing creates a comic effect from the implication that the speaker is incorrigibly accident-prone – each quatrain, by its last line, has him fired from each new job. Each time, however, Armitage finds a new phrase for being fired, drawing upon a stock of colloquial phrases that simultaneously reveals how large and various that stock actually is, and injects a vivid sense of a contemporary speaker. These effects of poetic voice are highly visible (or audible) in Armitage's poems and I dedicate a whole chapter, 'Armitage's Voices' to discussing them. So, here, each stanza's working of variations on the theme of being sacked builds momentum relentlessly, and that momentum is also impelled by other, more local variations. For example, there is a set worked around the motif of wood in the second stanza quoted here, which refers to carpentry, but also discovers metaphors relevant to the speaker's disastrous career, where wood is implicated in questions of joining and being ostracised, and finding yourself 'in lumber'. Critics of metaphysical poetry would call that a 'conceit', but in Armitage's hands it is exhilaratingly of the here and now and linked to a knowledge of contemporary music, with hints of a sort of 'hook' (Armitage's fondness for strategic repetition often suggests this too), and also with a post-punk sensibility of a 'never-mind-the-bollocks' kind.

The application of that attitude to literature explains much of Armitage's newness in the poetry world:

> bookish people imagine themselves as purists, but are actually perverts, belonging to a deviant culture. The appropriation of poetry by the literati can be quite properly compared with the enclosure of common land in England, the Highland Clearances and the hijacking of ancient medicine by Western science. We should never be surprised by the way in which the privileged minorities eventually take control of every valuable commodity, but how much more exciting it would have been

if poetry had been commandeered by people who did more than sit at home with their thumbs up their arses.[1]

That irreverent gusto is a key input into Armitage's poetry. He was not alone in this attitude, and his rise was aided by the presence of others who came to prominence in the late 80s, among them most notably Carol Ann Duffy who is eight years older than Armitage and was already establishing a reputation when Armitage's first book appeared (she was sufficiently established to be able to review it in *The Guardian*). Armitage had also been helped by the presence of poets from a similar background to himself (including Ian McMillan and Geoff Hattersley) and by the poetry scene in Huddersfield where Peter Sansom – who was important for many young poets – ran poetry workshops at the local polytechnic, and where Armitage and others (as he describes in *Gig*, pp.275–6) sat and wrote poems together in the Merrie England coffee houses (which he has celebrated in *Tyrannosaurus Rex versus The Corduroy Kid* pp. 21–3).

In my chapter 'Armitage's Contexts' I discuss wider settings for his work, including the precedents set by two key forefathers, W.H. Auden and Ted Hughes. Armitage's distinctiveness arises to some extent from his way of assimilating those canonical predecessors, which is to do with his interpolation of his own version of their themes into stylistic contexts invented partly through the example of two other influences – Paul Muldoon and Frank O'Hara. What must be stressed, however, is that crucial input into his sensibility comes from outside poetry altogether, from the kind of knowledge he brought to his poems from subject-matter which had previously not been prominent in poetry. I want to simplify here in order to stress this point: Armitage is a geography graduate, and he brought into poetry, whose orientation had been above all towards history, a geographical sensibility. I explore this at length firstly in 'Armitage's Contexts' and then in my last chapter 'Armitage's Changes of Place': his poetry represents a shift in paradigm from time to space. So his poems continuously express a spatial awareness which creates the particular kinds of specificity – of location and imagery – which are constitutive modes of expression in his work (including his novels and life writing, as well as his poems).

It is largely because Armitage's surfaces are so striking that his reviewers have sometimes implied that he lacks depth: but part of the point of his geographical sensibility is that his work is less about depth (as, for example, Seamus Heaney's is, with its obsession with wells and digging and archeological probing) than it is about extent, or extended surface. I would argue that this is one of the qualities that give his work depth in the metaphorical sense. And I have organised this book thematically in order to stress that Armitage is a considerable intellectual who tackles a wide range of issues which are of urgent contemporary import. One of these is gender; Armitage's focus on masculinity, which is the subject of my chapter 'Armitage: Man and Boy', is important because it still gets ignored as an explicit issue. Even now many university English departments teach modules, with 'Gender' in their titles, which are actually only about women – as though only women had a gender. That is troublingly sexist and does a disservice to women, because it implies that women are gendered whereas masculinity is universal. Armitage's reflections on masculinity are a consistent feature of all his writing, and he is especially acute about the drives and insecurities that fuel the most obsessive and off-handed, apparently gratuitously destructive behaviour.

What makes these reflections especially worth reading, though, is that they are almost always connected to another of the most distinctively Armitagean qualities – his affinity for the comic mode. I mean by this first of all that he is very funny, and it is one of the many drawbacks of literary criticism that it allows too little scope for conveying this quality, other than to keep repeating that the writing is funny, which does not work either. So I want to say here that often in this book I am describing texts which made me laugh but whose comedy I necessarily could not do justice to. However, I mean more than this. Armitage's rueful comedy often resembles that in satirical novelists like Joseph Heller and Philip Roth who test the edges of humour with a self-reflexiveness that draws attention to the interpenetration of comedy and seriousness – as, for example, in *Portnoy's Complaint*, where the central character declares himself to be living his life 'in the middle of the Jewish joke', declares that he is the son in the Jewish joke, '*only it ain't no joke!*' [2] Armitage's affinity for comedy is a characteristic feature of his sensibility in that he is drawn to its earthy, unpretentious idioms, and its exhilirating habit of dwelling on the possibilities of renewal and happy endings. Armitage often deals with grave themes but he always returns to the messages of comedy, including those of the most positive kind whose provenance dates from before the absurdism of Heller and Roth.

That makes the recent ecological turn in Armitage's writing especially promising. In the 'Afterword' to *The Poetry of Birds*, the anthology from 2009 which he co-edited with Tim Dee, Armitage writes that he started bird-watching when he stopped star-gazing:

> I swapped stars for birds, far livelier performers and creatures whose working hours coincided more conveniently with my own, i.e. daylight. Like my father, my bird-watching doesn't extend much beyond wanting to recognize something when it enters my field of vision, although I care enough about birds to be a card-carrying member of the million-strong RSPB, and I write poems about them as well.

Armitage's use of stars in *CloudCuckooLand* is abstract and metaphorical: by contrast his treatment of birds is much more direct and realistic. He has always notated flora and fauna, but his approach is now much more related to an ecological awareness whose background I describe in the last pages of this book. I am certain that this is a direction his work will increasingly take; but his fondness for the comic mode ensures that he will approach the subject with a vivid sense of how the ecocentric and the anthropocentric incongruously mingle, and of the still open possibilities for change and regeneration.

Notes

1. Simon Armitage, 'Re-Writing the Good Book' in W.N.Herbert and Matthew Hollis eds., *Strong Words: Modern Poets on Modern Poetry* (Highgreen, Tarset: Bloodaxe, 2000) p. 254.

2. Philip Roth, *Portnoy's Complaint* (London: Vintage, 1995) pp.36–7. First published 1967.

1

ARMITAGE'S CONTEXTS

In attempting to characterise the newness of contemporary poetry, critics have regularly called upon the concept of 'postmodernism', but the term is unhelpful unless it used carefully and with a willingness to make distinctions between writers who are thoroughly postmodernist and those who are merely, to a lesser or greater extent, influenced by the beliefs and strategies of postmodernism. Thorough postmodernists, such as John Ashbery, can be understood most accurately by reference to the concepts invented by Jacques Derrida to insist on the impossibility of ever reaching a stable position from which meaning can be finally determined – the concepts of deconstruction, decentring, supplementarity and free play. Derridean philosophy is a key input into postmodernist thought, and its dominant attitude is disbelief; deconstruction is disbelief put into practice; it is an anti-system, a system that subverts systems. Ashbery can be seen as emerging out of a surrealist tradition and as drawing upon surrealist tenets in order to express disbelief and to introduce subversive poetic modes which work deconstructively. Ashbery's surrealism involves endless defamiliarising; by contrast, British mainstream poets rely on evoking a sense of the real, however much they fracture and interrogate it, and on an underpinning of the familiar which produces greater stability. It is out of that latter tradition that Armitage emerges.

One way to define the postmodernity of a writer like Simon

Armitage is to define the extent to which he evidently comes after modernism. In Armitage's case, the most telling way to do this is to compare and contrast him with W.H. Auden – for, as reviewers of Armitage have repeatedly pointed out, there are conspicuous links between Auden and Armitage. Moreover, the differences between them are also highly symptomatic of changes that have taken place in poetry, and in the culture generally. Asked, in a profile of him in the special 'New Generation Poets' issue of *Poetry Review*, to name 'Three influential 20th C. books', Armitage named Auden's *Collected Poems*, Ted Hughes's *Selected Poems*, and Robert Lowell's *Life Studies*[1] – where Auden is honoured above the other two by being the only one represented by his complete poetic canon. Armitage was asked to commemorate the Travelling Post Office when its services were no longer required, and he recalls Auden's 'Night Mail', which was also about the TPO, and declares his affinity with his predecessor:

> Auden saw himself as a poet who could turn his hand to any kind of verse, whether it be the most intricate formal sequence intended for a literary publication or a casual rhyme for a friend's birthday. I'm of a similar mind, holding the view that any situation or scene can be expressed as poetry (*Gig*, p.41).

This attitude has loomed with increasing importance in Armitage's career, as he has responded to an increasing number of commissions.

W.H. Auden and Simon Armitage, as I discuss in 'Armitage's Changes of Place', share a preoccupation with place and landscape. Their landscapes, moreover, are rarely single and isolated but almost always related to a knowledge of elsewhere because twentieth-century modes of communication and transport, and systems of exchange, result in places intermingling and interpenetrating. The consequent unsettling of place arouses anxiety and anger in Auden, and he repeatedly diagnoses the causes as lying in capitalism – which he systematically attacks. That unsettling of place is a constituent part of Armitage's sensibility, and a key source of his imagery and defamilirising strategies, but it is accepted by him as inevitable and sometimes even celebrated and enjoyed. Auden starts with an objective diagnosis of the condition, but, as his career progresses, increasingly reacts against it by expressing nostalgia for lost places and by dwelling on a fantasy of Eden, of a guiltless setting immune to Time. This is a key difference between modernist poets – who share a tendency to indict capitalism and to long for a pre-capitalist state which was 'natural' and free of alienation – and postmodern poets. Armitage never expresses anything like this sense of loss; his childhood landscapes are repeatedly evoked, and regarded nostalgically, but his poetry is mostly lacking in mythic depths (except for a brief period when, in *Dead Sea Scrolls*, he hankered after myth).

In reacting against the unsettling of place, by contrast, Auden's poems repeatedly return to the 'private sacred world' which he constructed in childhood and whose basic elements were 'a landscape, northern and limestone, and an industry, lead mining'.[2] The personal meaning of that world is less acknowledged in his earliest work and is more explicit in the mid–30s and after when he is less influenced by modernist impersonality and more prepared, especially in his long poems, to expatiate on his own experience. He recalls, in 'Letter to Lord Byron', his admiration for a coalfield he saw from a train on the line between Birmingham and Wolverhampton: aged four, he was envious of scenery which included tramlines and slagheaps. In 'New Year Letter' he broadens the landscape of his geographical nostalgia to include the limestone moors between Brough and Hexham (anticipating his more famous 'In Praise of Limestone') and a Tyne and Wear region of derelict mills and mines.

The mythologizing of this theme by turning it into a process in which innocent settings are made to resemble Eden, and then shown to be damaged, is characteristic of modernism, and is part of the modernist preoccupation with archaeological depths. Those depths are symptomatically lacking in a postmodern poet like Armitage – though, as I will show later in this chapter, they are replaced with other features more expressive of the postmodern condition. For Auden, the damaging of innocent settings is associated with that devastation of pastoral recorded in the poetry of the First World War. In the 'charade' *Paid on Both Sides*, first published in 1930, the warring of two mill-owning families in the north of England is taken to exemplify the violence made inevitable by capitalism, which performs a grotesque parody of Nature. Foundries and shops acquire renewed energy in Spring, but the culture of war is insinuated everywhere. Pararhyme makes *Paid on Both Sides* echo with the memory of Wilfred Owen's Spring offensives. The eventual failure of Spring, however, is reminiscent of the diagnosis, in *The Waste Land*, of a degenerate spiritual condition in which Spring is symptomatically damaged, but it is reinterpreted by Auden in Marxist terms as the consequence of the contradictions of capitalism which drives an overproduction that leads to systemic breakdown.

The fantasy of returning to a place which is immune to Time, which is natural and eternal and so beyond human law, underlies much of Auden's work and becomes increasingly explicit. It is so powerful for him that he assumes that every writer must share it and that, while a novelist or poet need not divulge his private Eden, 'the moment he starts writing criticism, honesty demands that he describes it to his readers'. [3] So he presents, as a necessary prologue to his other essays in *The Dyer's Hand*, a list of the kinds of landscape, climate, and so on which would constitute his Eden. It is evidently a premise of such a landscape that it represents a lost state, because its energy sources will not include oil, its modes of transport will include horses, railways and canals but no cars or planes, and its public entertainments will consist of religious processions, brass bands, opera and classical ballet, but no films, radio or television.

Those references amplify the meaning of Eden in Auden's poems because they are combined with an analysis of the impact of capitalism on the 'social conception of time' (*Dyer's Hand*, p.220). In his critique of *The Merchant of Venice* he focuses on the contrast between the historical reality of Venice, with its money-making, and 'the romantic fairy-story world of Belmont', but thinks that the play is unpleasant because it compels its audience to question its attraction to Belmont and its claim to be 'the Great Good Place, the Earthly Paradise' (p.221).Venice depends upon its profits from international trade and so exemplifies the profound change in sensibility which arises as a result of the economic shift from 'landownership to money capital':

> The wealth produced by land may vary from year to year – there are good harvests and bad – but, in the long run its average yield may be counted upon. Land, barring dispossession by an invader or confiscation by the State, is held by a family in perpetuity. In consequence, the social conception of time in a landowning society is cyclical – the future is expected to be a repetition of the past. But in a mercantile society time is conceived of as unilinear forward movement in which the future is always novel and unpredictable. (p.220)

Belmont, by this account, exists in a different time to Venice, it is a fairy-tale place which is 'a world of being not becoming': for Auden its questioning contrasts with the more congenial sanctioning of Falstaff's world of 'opera buffa' in *Henry IV*. Its unpleasantness, however, resembles that of his own poem 'No Change of Place', which also defies its own historical period with an atavistic, landowning stasis: it derives from the undermining of the fantasy of return to the Great Good Place, the denial of the wish-fulfilling alternative to the lapsarian state of capitalism, the dream turning into nightmare. The unpleasantness is especially acute for Auden because he regards the 'unilinear forward movement' of capitalism with such horror.

It is characteristic of postmodern poets that they represent a cultural condition which is so thoroughly inside capitalism that no diagnosis, such as this, of a state preceding it, and of a process that led from that into capitalism, appears possible. Armitage's postmodernity is evident from the way that he is similar to Auden in exploring the meanings of place (and they share Yorkshire places in common) but symptomatically differs from him in being uninterested in large-scale historical explanations for why the concept of place has been systemically altered. For a poet such as Armitage being 'anti-capitalist' would appear to be a posture on too large a scale, too philosophically ambitious – it would seem pretentious.

Ted Hughes, like Auden, is a pre-postmodern poet who traces historical processes and represents them in mythic terms. He is another poet with whom Armitage shares a formative affinity, although, again, he does not share the mythic, or even the historical, dimension of his predecessor. In an early interview, Armitage is asked what made him start writing and he says:

> I think it was being homesick, because the things that I wrote were about round here, and I remember going into a bookshop and buying Ted Hughes' *Selected Poems*. I thought it would remind me of home – we'd done him at school, and he was the guy who lived over the other side of the hill. [4]

In his 'Introduction' to his selection of the poetry of Ted Hughes, Armitage makes similar points about his connections with Hughes, especially the regional connection, referring to Hughes as a man who felt 'nostalgia' for the same place as himself, though he also reflects that that place had a different 'meaning' for each of them (p.xv). Hughes is important to Armitage as a more recent, and much more impressive, local poet than Samuel Laycock who Armitage refers to in two poems, and also in his life writing (see my chapter 'Armitage's Voices'). As such Hughes provides a role model and it is significant that Armitage mentions, again in that 'Introduction', meeting Hughes several times at poetry readings. The nature of his identification takes on gender as well as regional characteristics and it is noticeable that in Armitage's second novel, *The White Stuff*, which reflects repeatedly on men and masculinity, the protagonist's wife Abbie tells her husband that women are adaptable and didn't need to support the nearest football team, or go drinking in a 'local', or get into fights with people from other parts of the country because they spoke differently, or have the name of their home town tattooed across their hearts. Men thought about their place of birth in the same way they thought about their mothers – with unquestioning affection. They were tied down and they were trapped. (p. 21)

This is the view of a female character with a particular bias: she was adopted, and never thought of Norfolk, where she grew up, as home. Nonetheless it has a particular relevance for Armitage, who has always felt a strong affinity with his native village of Marsden in West Yorkshire, and has been continually preoccupied with the nature of masculinity.

Ted Hughes is an important model for Armitage in both these respects, as a male poet from West Yorkshire who wrote about that region, and whose thinking had a key gender dimension. Hughes's development involved his increasing awareness of the gender issue; he moved from the shaping, in his early work, of his own forms of masculine expression, to an explicit questioning of gender and to regretting what he diagnosed as a masculine drive to repudiate the feminine. The gender aspect of Hughes's early poems becomes clear when they are contrasted with those by his wife Sylvia Plath. Hughes's natural images, like the hawk in 'Hawk Roosting', express rigid and steely self-containment: Plath's express leakage and liquefaction; where Hughes chooses a hawk as a dramatic monologuist, Plath chooses an elm: the man/predator is a masterful monolith, the woman/elm is anxiously multiple and fragmented. In *Wodwo* (1967) and after, Hughes's gender self-consciousness grows, and he increasingly adopts an ideology derived partly from Robert Graves's *The White Goddess* but also connected to the anthropological theories behind T.S.Eliot's *The Waste Land* which refer to the idea of sacrifices made to a fertility goddess. Eliot's poem grieves over the loss of that source of regeneration and implicitly relates it to the loss of Christian belief: Hughes's version focuses, via Graves, more on the loss of the feminine principle, and locates it historically in the movement away from Catholicism, with its focus on the Virgin, and into Protestantism. This becomes his key idea: Protestantism, which is also associated with capitalism, represents a systemic rejection of the feminine which inflicts dire consequences on Western culture. Hughes saw this as the constitutive theme of Shakespeare's work, and the central thesis of his *Shakespeare and the Goddess of Complete*

Being[5] is that Shakespeare's whole oeuvre is shaped around a core myth – Venus and Adonis – which elaborately grieves over this loss. He attempts in this book to show how the Adonis myth expresses a rejection of the feminine caused by boyhood resentment and fear of the mother's power:

> The peculiar division of the sexes, which bestows on woman the miraculous power to create man out of her blood, while it deprives man of any such ability, and which deposits the infant male, through his helpless, formative years, into the possessive control of the Female, injects a peculiar conflict into the situation.

This leads Hughes to see the rejection of the feminine as the root explanation of the overly masculine, rationalist culture of Protestantism and capitalism, and the emphasis of both his Shakespeare book and his later poetry is to heal the violent divisiveness that arises from the 'peculiar conflict' between the sexes. It is in *Crow*, in particular, that Hughes diagnoses the sickness – that sequence is dominated by the themes of gender conflict and division, and brilliantly examines the damage caused by the attempts of masculinity to define itself against, and establish its independence from, femininity. What is most importantly missing is the creative and regenerative spirit of the feminine: *Crow* everywhere explores the consequences of the repudiation of the Goddess, who is referred to directly in 'Crow's Undersong', where she is depicted as constantly trying to travel towards us but not quite arriving, so that she is just under our threshold of apprehension.

These mythic ideas are very alien to Simon Armitage, and in *Killing Time* he explicitly ridicules New Age types who want to chat with the 'Mother Goddess' on a mobile phone (p.10). Nonetheless, he does share Hughes's preoccupation with masculinity, and Armitage's parody of *Crow* provides a clue in this respect to Hughes's importance for the younger poet: 'Not the Furniture Game' (*Kid*, pp.66–7) is focused on exactly the gender preoccupations I have been describing, and provides the correct context for my discussion of Armitage's gender preoccupations in the chapter 'Man and Boy'. The poem's title refers to the game in which a character must be described in terms of what other phenomena they would most resemble: if the character was a piece of furniture, or a season of the year, or a fruit, etc. – what would they be? The character in this case, however, is not a person but a personification of the masculinity which *Crow* indicts as ignorantly destructive; bits of his body are separately named and then compared to a series of objects which are very diverse but share in common a phallic, and sometimes violent, hardness – boiled eggs with their ends bashed in, a ball cock, a broken bottle. This might be related to a twentieth-century tradition in poetry derived from Imagism, whose tenets, as propounded by Ezra Pound, opposed impressionistic deliquessence and advocated an unyielding hardness which would mean that juxtaposed objects would define each other by contrast and so aid the projecting of images on the reader's mind. That male tradition gave priority to the sort of hard images that bristle in this poem, but here their hardness is inflected explicitly towards the gender issue, and linked to others with wider associations; a heart which is a hand grenade found by children, a navel which is the Falkland Islands, footprints which are Vietnam – these all refer to the point which Hughes repeatedly makes (but most explicitly in 'A Motorbike') about a drive towards war which is programmed into male hormones. The horror that keeps erupting throughout the poem indicates why it is 'not' the furniture game, but the title acquires special relevance at the point where a female character enters: having said that the last conversation between the man and the woman was 'apartheid', and so alluding to Hughes's idea of the damage caused by the repudiation of the feminine, Armitage describes the woman as 'a chair', but with the implication, opposing the furniture game, that she has only become a domestic object because of the oppressive influence of her male partner, whose heavy jacket on her shoulders drags her to the floor.

Auden and Hughes are crucial for Armitage thematically and I have dedicated a chapter each (respectively 'Changes of Place' and

'Man and Boy') to the themes in Armitage's work where these prede-cessors are most important. Stylistically, however, these poets are a less conspicuous influence than others, especially Paul Muldoon and Frank O'Hara. John Redmond says that Armitage's 'early style owed a lot to Paul Muldoon: a combination of unreliable narrators, renewed clichés, off-rhymes, colloquial vagueness and black humour.'[6] Apart from the gratuitous dig in 'vagueness', which is characteristic of Redmond's hauteur in his *Cambridge Companion* essay, his summary of Muldoon's input into Armitage's work is accurate, and relates to the effects of dialogic novelisation which I discuss in 'Armitage's Voices'. Muldoon, with his hybrid mingling of textual materials, his multiplying of registers and genres, his parodic tendency to site his poems hesitantly between different discourses, provided a model for poets after him to play fast and loose with all stabilities of voice, and that model was crucial for Armitage who derives so much of his dis-tinctiveness from his invention of an energetic range of colloquial expression.

Like Muldoon, Frank O'Hara has been a liberating influence for contemporary poets, and largely because he opposes any sense of the self as in any way rigidly identifiable, and presents it – especially in his 'I do this, I do that' poems – being invented in the process of what it does. O'Hara's most famous poems present him in his lunch hour wandering through the streets of New York and so showing a self in process, which is why cinema and action painting are accu-rate analogues for his work. 'The Day Lady Died' and 'A Step away from Them', for example, are radically existential in that they pre-sent a notion of the self as composed minute by minute. They share that existentialism with contemporaries of O'Hara's such as Robert Lowell, John Berryman, and Sylvia Plath, but they are entirely lack-ing in the existential angst which is such a feature of confessional writing, and are determined to avoid portentousness and to carry their subject-matter lightly – even when it becomes anxious, as it does sometimes about whether it is possible to discern any meaning at all in the overwhelmingly trivial nature of 1950s New York life. The lack of angst, and the emphasis on enjoyment, even of trivia, are key components for Armitage, who has described himself as 'a person whose mood indicator rarely swings below the contentment line and is more often than not up at the happiness end of the dial;' (*Gig*, p.181). Like Muldoon, therefore, O'Hara provided a model of how to write poems which were exhilaratingly open-ended and fun, where the fun did not preclude a sense that important themes were being tackled.

The context in which Armitage started to write was dominated by a poetic in which figures such as Muldoon and O'Hara were representative. In grieving over the death of his friend Michael Donaghy, Armitage has characterised that context as 'the new buoyancy in poetry during the late eighties and early nineties'. Taking Donaghy as an exemplar of that mood he says:

> He was a communicator who loved an audience. On the page, with one choice phrase, he could bridge the worlds of philosophy and popular culture. I even heard that he liked to write standing at a lectern, as if the final delivery of the poem was never far from his mind. (*Gig*, p.116)

The group of writers who rose to prominence in that period, who included Carol Ann Duffy, Glyn Maxwell, Don Paterson and Kathleen Jamie, and have since come to be called the New Generation, did have important differences from the ones who were already established, and Armitage's reference to popular culture is an important clue. There was certainly a sense that intellectual hierarchies were being called into question, and there is some accuracy in the claim by Peter Forbes (editor at the time of *Poetry Review*) that the new poets represented a move away from an Oxford hegemony represented by Ian Hamilton and James Fenton, [7] and that this was to some extent the product of a 'social atomization' Britain had undergone in the 1980s, in which

> The centre could not hold in anything. Private worlds, subcults, proliferated. The central channels of literary culture,

the BBC, Oxbridge, Penguin books, Faber & Faber, the *New Statesman* and *The Listener*, all had to adapt to being just one player amongst several. One of these has already foundered and others may follow. It became less likely that any two people would have seen the same TV programme, read the same book, or share any culture at all in a meaningful sense. (p.4)

By far the best account of the complex origins and nature of the New Generation, though, is in *New Relations* by David Kennedy; his account of the poetry of Simon Armitage and Glyn Maxwell as the product of a 'rhetorical imagination', which reflects its cultural origins, remains persuasive. He identifies, in particular, an erosion of consensus, and a commodifying of history, leading to a loss of an historical self, a disconnection between the poet's personal voice and that of his native language, and an increasing sense of 'isolation and discontinuity':

What results is an imagination that places its emphasis on and draws its energy from the forms rather than the noise of language; that is not auditory but rhetorical. I have, however, used the conditional tense in the preceding account because while the rhetorical imagination can be described as the product of an impoverishment, it would be wholly incorrect to assume that it is itself a form of impoverishment. Indeed, one of the paradoxes of the poetry of both Simon Armitage and Glyn Maxwell is that carefully husbanded resources of containment and circumspection go hand-in-hand with exuberant enjoyment, prolific output and a wide range of occasion and inspiration. [8]

The cultural impoverishment which Kennedy describes can be seen as part of a general postmodern sensibility which Fredric Jameson has explained by reference to his concept of 'depthlessness', which involves the loss of four 'depth models' which were characteristic of modernism: essence versus appearance; the Freudian unconscious;

the existential distinction between the authentic and the inauthentic; and the structuralist opposition between the signifier and the signified. 9 This depthlessness is linked to other losses: the withering away of Nature; the loss of historical consciousness; and the 'waning of affect' (p. 10). A comparison between Armitage and his two major predecessors reveals key differences of this kind; the lack of the mythic dimension can also be seen as a loss of depth, and it is joined by another because both Auden and Hughes diagnose the modern predicament by reference to historical processes resulting from capitalism – but in Armitage this diagnosis is entirely lacking. David Kennedy is evidently surprised that poets such as Armitage and Maxwell can be so richly expressive when they seem so lacking in historical consciousness and he manages to find a partial explanation for that. However, there is another which is actually simpler than his – which is that they replace historical consciousness with other kinds of consciousness, and ones which are particularly exciting because they are representative of contemporary culture. The obvious one is popular culture and all of the New Generation poets are more in sympathy with television and cinema and contemporary music than older contemporaries such as Seamus Heaney, Tony Harrison, Craig Raine and Andrew Motion. But it goes deeper than this. Very few of the New Generation poets write literary criticism, whereas Auden, Hughes, Heaney, Raine and most of the others did, and these new poets are intellectuals of a different sort, and have expertise in areas other than ones that twentieth-century poets tended to have as their primary expertise, which was in history, and the history of literature and art, and to some extent in politics and philosophy.

The loss of this consciousness may look like a loss of depth, but it is actually the negative part in a shift of paradigm in poetry which replaces depth with extent, the vertical with the horizontal – or time with space. That shift would please the postmodern geographer Edward Soja who has lamented the privileging of history in Western thought, which therefore produces an historicism which is an 'overdeveloped . . . contextualization of social life and social theory that actively submerges and peripheralizes the geographical or spatial imagination.'[10] It is that previously marginalized imagination which now looms in poetry much larger than it did, and which is especially conspicuous in Simon Armitage who has a geography degree, and who was in a defensive mood when he wrote about his first book for the Poetry Book Society's quarterly *Bulletin*:

> From the word go I've indulged in all the wrong subjects: Geography, Politics, Sociology, Psychology, even Oceanography, and although I couldn't have written half of *Zoom!* without such a broad skim of knowledge, I can't help thinking there are greater things to know about; better books to have read.[11]

The spatial element in Armitage's metaphor 'broad skim' confirms the point; he is anxious that his knowledge is superficial – that it spreads out rather than digs down – and that it is wrong because it is not primarily literary-historical. But it is actually one of the most important keys to his distinctiveness as a writer. In his second book, *Xanadu*, which was about the Ashfield Valley Estate in Rochdale, where he had his first posting as a probation officer, he represents the very stark urban conditions, but he also transforms them with references to very different places, such as Manderley, and Xanadu itself, and by asking fundamental (and geographically educated) questions about the concept of place:

A million books
don't make it clearer,
a thousand years
and we're still no nearer.

all that guff
about place and space,
an ocean of stuff
and it's still a case

of ip dip dip,

my blue ship,
which came first

the flea or the pit?
which makes which,
the pig or the sty?
all that time

and we're still not certain,
what wears what,
the brick or the person?

Armitage's knowledge of geography mingles, in these lines, with his knowledge of sociology as he asks the often repeated questions about place and identity. And, as I show in 'Armitage's Changes of Place', the crucial specificities in his writing – which often focus on identity questions – are achieved through his mapping ability, his awareness of spatial relationships, so that his images are pinpointed in relation to each other by linguistic map references. Armitage's 'The Personal Touch' (*Seeing Stars*, pp. 55–6) is partly a joke about this issue: its speaker asks his partner what she would like for their first anniversary, and she replies that she wants some 'space', so he goes out to a hardware store to buy some, and is offered space from a range of origins, including from the ocean and the Antarctic, and from outer space.

The spatial elements in Armitage are linked to the most conspicuous recent development in his work – his growing concern with ecological issues. Here the context is one which has arisen while Armitage's writing career has been underweigh, and involves recent developments in cultural history and environmental politics. Nature-bashing was prevalent in the 1980s: it was claimed that the cultural condition of late capitalism was postmodernism, which was what happens 'when Nature is gone for good' (*Jameson*, p. ix). Deconstruction was founded upon suspicion of claims of naturalness, and upon Derrida's critique of Heidegger, the major existentialist philosopher of being in relation to Nature; Walter Abish, similarly, published a novel, *How German Is It*, which was ruefully ironic about the German habit of wandering off into the countryside, and which contained a character very like Heidegger, who was complicit with the Nazis. Literary critics on the left, like Jerome McGann and Marilyn Butler, deconstructed a 'Romantic ideology' which they said involved a retreat from the pressing concerns of capitalist society into consolations which were escapist and reactionary.

The 1990s, however, saw a shift from suspicion of Nature to a renewed focus on the biosphere arising, in particular, from escalating anxieties about the consequences of environmental damage, and especially about the increasing evidence of climate change. Lawrence Buell, in the USA, and Jonathan Bate in Britain, led the way in inventing 'ecocriticism', which explored the relationship between literature and Nature: Buell was especially brilliant on Thoreau, Bate on Wordsworth. In this context, the work of contemporary nature poets has acquired a newly urgent meaning, and in placing himself sometimes among their number, Armitage once again has a very specific positioning in relation to postmodernism. The greatest poem of the twentieth century, *The Waste Land*, was focused about the damage to Nature caused by urbanisation and industrialisation, and upon the alienation of modern people from natural cycles and seasonal rhythms, and it initiated a tradition of such poetry. Postmodernism, by contrast, is urban and metropolitan, Frank O'Hara declared that he was never comfortable unless there was a subway handy, and this camp anti-Nature stance is characteristically postmodern. Simon Armitage may have proclaimed himself, when recounting his visit to Baltimore, O'Hara's birthplace, a 'Frank O'phile from an early age',[12] and he may have drawn upon that influence in order to help him construct an apparently urban poetic, but his poetry has always been interested in the places where the natural and the urban overlap. And here as elsewhere, Armitage's position in relation to postmodernism is that he deals with the political and cultural issues but does so in a style which is influenced by postmodernist scepticism while retaining the underpinning of crucial stabilities. So, as I show at the end of 'Armitage's Changes of Place', he engages fully with the threats to nature and the consequent challenges with which all ecopoets are preoccupied.

Notes

1. *Poetry Review*, Spring 1994, p.8.

2. W.H. Auden, *Forewards and Afterwords* (London: Faber, 1973) p.502.

3. W.H. Auden, *The Dyer's Hand and Other Essays* (London: Faber, 1962) p.6. This volume henceforth *Dyer's Hand*.

4. Chris Greenhalgh, 'Simon Armitage: An Interview with Chris Greenhalgh', *Bete Noire*, Autumn 1991/Spring 1992, p. 261.

5. Ted Hughes, *Shakespeare and the Goddess of Complete Being* (London: Faber, 1992) p.327.

6. John Redmond, 'Lyric adaptations: James Fenton, Craig Raine, Christopher Reid, Simon Armitage, Carol Ann Duffy' in Neil Corcoran ed., *The Cambridge Companion to Twentieth-Century English Poetry* (Cambridge: Cambridge University Press, 2007) p.254. Redmond's over-confidence is exposed when, in a discussion of 'Five Eleven Ninety Nine', he refers to a 'Hallowe'en bonfire' (p. 257).

7. Peter Forbes, 'Talking About the New Generation: Peter Forbes on the new, the old, and "the last gasp of a system of patronage" ' *Poetry Review* Spring 1994, pp.4–6.

8. David Kennedy, *New Relations: The Refashioning of British Poetry 1980–94* (Bridgend: Seren, 1996) p.59.

9. Fredric Jameson, *Postmodernism, Or, The Cultural Logic of Late Capitalism* (London: Verso, 1991), p.12. This book henceforth *Jameson*.

10. Edward Soja, *Postmodern Geographies: The Reassertion of Space in Critical Social Theory*, (London: Verso, 1989) p. 15.

11. Simon Armitage, 'Simon Armitage' in Clare Brown and Don Paterson eds., *Don't Ask me What I Mean: Poets in their Own Words* (Basingstoke: Macmillan, 2003) p.4.

12. Simon Armitage, 'Armitage in America', *Poetry Review*, Spring 1994, p.11.

2

ARMITAGE'S VOICES

WHEN HE FIRST started to publish, Simon Armitage grabbed attention above all because of the edginess and energy of his poetic voice, which seemed unprecedently to make poetically available something contemporary which was altogether from outside the literary world, as though he had managed to introduce something directly from contemporary life. There is some truth in this first impression, because Armitage's experience, as a young man, as a probation officer, had given him access to experiences which were unavailable to other writers. *All Points North* describes how he 'worked with one lad who got stabbed in the small of his back trying to swipe a bag of heroin from his dealer. He didn't go to hospital till he was shitting out of the hole, three days later.'(p.8) His poem 'The Dragon', from *CloudCuckooLand*, is the poetic version of that incident, in which the small of the back becomes 'the arse' (p. 33) and so illustrates the process through which the raw material is translated into poetry.

The first poem in Armitage's first book, 'Snow Joke' (*Zoom!*, p.9) announces him by using the bad pun in its title to pretend to tick the poem off for its playful heartlessness, its enjoyment of its own narrative panache, which is felt even at the expense of its central character. The aspect of this which helped Armitage become famous was the synergy between the late 80s content and his style: the dead man's over-confident driving resembles the poet's look-no-hands story-telling, his witty and self-conscious facility. Nonetheless, it is easy to see why poems like this can be read as vividly authentic, as spoken in a voice which Peter Sansom in the book's blurb describes as 'really his *own* voice – his language and rhythms drawn from the Pennine village where he lives: robust, no-nonsense and (above all) honest'. The speaker declares his own no-nonsense robustness in telling the story of an accidental death in a tone of dispassionate dismissiveness, or even *schadenfreude* motivated by jealousy towards the victim's wealth and sexual success – enjoying a come-uppance inflicted upon a hubristic ignoring of a police warning about a blizzard – so that the victim was found 'slumped against the steering wheel/ with VOLVO printed backwards in his frozen brow.' It is this steadfast refusal of sympathy which gives the poem its apparently anti-poetic demeanour, or that combined with the earthy practicality of the men sharing the story, men with thorough knowledge of the roads, and the region, in which the accident happened. This is also Armitage's knowledge, made evident, again, in *All Points North* where he describes the M62:

> Thousands of tons of steel pass any given point every minute of the day, but when the winter brings the motorway to a frozen standstill, convoys are snuffed out by the snow in less than an hour, and vehicles are excavated weeks later like woolly mammoths out of the tundra. (p.16)

Another characteristic of Armitage's early voice which was especially striking was its youthfulness: readers were impressed by this but also a little unnerved – so Philip Gross, in a review of *Kid* in 1992, said

> Simon Armitage's off-the-cuff manner, his speedy street-credible delivery, leaves me feeling middle-aged. Then again, it's meant to. Anyone who calls their first book *Zoom!* And their second *Kid* must be toying with the label *whizzkid*. And so he is, with just enough self-mockery to let us know he might be only, yes, kidding. [1]

There is an element of authenticity, as there is in Armitage's other vocal effects, in the youthful noises which his early poems make. He was still in his twenties when he published his first three books, and he was knowledgeable about youth culture. Gross is astute, though, in his choice of that word 'kidding' – the pun is brilliantly appropriate in indicating the combination of genuine youthfulness with the self-conscious parodying of a role. Armitage's kidding is one of his key achievements because it introduced into poetry a vivid representation of a distinctive characteristic of postmodern culture – its preoccupation with a speed of cultural change which meant that generational shifts were being accelerated and generational differences becoming increasingly marked and focused upon. Some of the kidding comes directly from life and is that kind of material which Graham Mort, reviewing *Zoom*, refers to when he claims that a 'number of poems are constructed entirely from conversational snippets overheard at work or on buses'. [2]

Some of the kidding even seems to come directly from Armitage's own life; 'Missed It by That Much' and 'Potassium' (*Zoom!*, pp. 31, 56–7) read plausibly like accounts of the poet's own early sexual experiences. 'Missed It by That Much' describes a bike ride into the countryside where the boy and girl pick fruit from a hedgerow, then free-wheel into a valley through the smoke of burning stubble; what he most remembers, though, is the pair of them 'dropping like two cut flowers', where the image carries associations of burgeoning sexuality, but also of a sudden curtailment confirmed by the idea (returning to the cycling) that 'The rest was all downhill.' There are hints of 'paysage moralisé' which lead to that topographical cliché and renew it – the pair look post-coitally at landmarks down below, and then they stand, with the girl leaning against a trig-point – so that the place is made to represent a time and a rite of passage. 'Potassium' comes from earlier in the poet's life, when he was thirteen and kissed a girl who was the same age, and there is less of the epiphanic in his account, and more of the random: the surrounding events are tangential, especially the eponymous feeding – by a man who is later arrested – of the metal to gulls, which makes them explode. The tangential presentation of the material works like a guarantee of authenticity, it produces a 'reality effect' by its apparent evasion of literary selection and structuring.

Armitage has also written poems with school settings, as in 'Newton's Third Law', which is about a glamorous couple of lesbians whose interest in each other sets them apart from the childish spitefulness and cruelty of their schoolmates, and who are caught by the head of physics

testing

their charge on the gold-leaf meter after
kissing the Van der Graaf generator.   (*Zoom!*,p.15)

The alienness of the girls, as perceived by the other pupils, is evoked by their association with an exotic piece of scientific apparatus, whose name, by including the word 'generator', with its distant hint of sexuality, also suggests what happens when those pupils try to understand gay activity. Elsewhere, the school poems are explicitly presented as Armitage's own experience, but they similarly draw upon the knowledge learned in school as an equivalent to an adolescent striving to understand the world. 'You May Turn Over and Begin . . .' (*Kid*, pp.19–20) treats the idea lightly by describing a schoolboy's frustration at the preference of his schoolgirl contemporaries for older males, and expressing it by juxtaposing an account of 'A' level General Studies and a maliciously enjoyed story about how one of these girls, on her boyfriend's Honda, put both feet on the ground at some traffic lights and was stranded there, and how he, not realising, 'underbalanced' on a corner and ended up unconscious in an ambulance. One of the General Studies questions quoted at the start is made relevant by being answered at the end after the telling of this story: *A Taste of Honey* is also a story of youthful sexuality, and the implied schoolboy knowledge gained (simultaneously from life and from cinema) is the difference between the sexual mores of the 1950s and that of the 1980s. The striving for understanding is more urgent in 'Revision Exercise with Textbook Examples' (*Kid*, pp. 69–70) which can be read, *pace* Wordsworth, as a synecdochic account of the growth of the poet's mind because it represents what will become a characteristic Armitage strategy of defamiliarising in which exotic imagery is juxtaposed with the local and apparently mundane. The lesson is geography, which, as I will explore further in the chapter 'Armitage's Changes of Place', is one of the poet's major preoccupations, and this poem prefigures his habit of panning and zooming, of moving from tight enclosures into massively large spaces, in order to reveal the astonishing oddness inside the everyday. The poem concludes by imagining a terrace of houses that straddles the equator, so that at its northern end the water circles clockwise around the plughole, circles anti-clockwise at the southern end, – and, in the house that sits on the equator, sinks vertically.

Above all, however, Armitage's kidding is a carefully calculated effect and can be compared to that kind of first-person narration used in *Huckleberry Finn* and *Catcher in the Rye* which is referred to as 'teenage *skaz*': the manner is thoroughly oral, it is colloquial and apparently spontaneous, and, as David Lodge has said, creates 'a powerful effect of authenticity and sincerity, of truth-telling.'[3] Lodge's account of Holden Caulfield's narrative voice is especially relevant to Armitage's early manner:

> There's a lot of repetition (because elegant variation in vocabulary requires careful thought) especially of slang expressions ... Like many young people, Holden expresses the strength of his feelings by exaggeration ... The syntax is simple. Sentences are typically short and uncomplicated. Many of them aren't properly formed, lacking a finite verb ... There are grammatical mistakes such as speakers often make ... In longer sentences, clauses are strung together as they seem to occur to the speaker, rather than being subordinated to each other in complex structures. (p.19)

That description is especially appropriate for the voice of 'Kid' itself, for there the accent is American and self-consciously fictive, being Robin talking to Batman:

> Holy robin-redbreast-nest-egg-shocker!
> Holy roll-me-over-in-the-clover,
> I'm not playing ball boy any longer
> Batman, now I've doffed that off-the-shoulder
> Sherwood-Forest-green and scarlet number
> For a pair of jeans and crew-neck jumper;   (p.36)

There is a linguistic struggle in these lines between authenticity and fiction, which mirrors Robin's own struggle to be authentic, to cease being a cartoon. The mingling of registers – Batman exclamatory mode ('Holy' this and that), newspaper headline ('shocker), and song lyric – and the mingling of Batman with Robin Hood, both enact Robin's own sense of a chaotic identity which he has now cast off in achieving a stable 1950s American style represented by his new clothes.

The struggle of a cartoon character to become authentic has a representative significance for Armitage – and, more broadly for contemporary British poetry in the 1990s. Much of the debate surrounding Armitage's earliest work involves his supporters proclaiming his honesty and others doubting it. On the blurb to *Zoom!*, Carol Ann Duffy is quoted in a review from *The Guardian* praising Armitage for writing 'poems with an energy which comes directly from life now and the living language.' On the other hand the eminent literary critic John Bayley declared that 'Simon Armitage and other virtuoso performers have acquired the postmodernist trick of putting poetry, like a clever TV advertisement, in inverted commas, of being clever whilst amusing us about the process of being clever, using cliché or romance with a streetwise grin'. [4] Armitage's own view is that he is telling stories; in *All Points North* he repeatedly reveals how the process of story-telling works so that it involves both truth and fiction. When he and his fellow thespians (in an amateur theatre group directed by Armitage's father) are returning after a performance in Bridlington, they tell school stories on the bus:

> How Mrs Dyson made Terry Pamment piss his britches by saying, 'You *can* go to the toilet, but you *may* not.' How Jumbo Ellis and his mates broke into the school, and Ellis got stuck in the window, trapping them all inside like a cork.
>
> 'He was ginormous,' says someone.
> 'He's dead,' says someone else.
> How a fifth-former threw half a dozen hens into the school one night, followed by a fox.
> 'That true?'
> 'Nope,' says the person telling the story.' (p.36)

Earlier in that book (pp.8–9) he tells equally apocryphal stories about his experiences as a probation officer, but his kidding technique involves telling the story first, and only revealing its untruth as a punchline: 'Actually that story isn't true, but people told it so many times you started to believe it happened to you.' (p.9)

Much of the impression of authenticity comes from a belief that speech is more 'true' than text; the blurb quotations from Peter Sansom and Carol Ann Duffy both contain this assumption, with Sansom proclaiming an organic link between Armitage's voice and 'the Pennine village where he lives', and Duffy stressing the 'living language', where the implication is that it is only oral language which is truly alive. It is because Armitage is so adept at imitating speech that he arouses this response; the voice in 'Snow Joke' is presented as a man telling a joke, and its rhythms are precisely timed to follow the rushes and hesitations of a story being told face to face, with 'Well,' ending the first stanza. 'Very Simply Topping Up the Brake Fluid' (*Zoom*, p.30), similarly, mimics a mechanic painstakingly explaining the eponymous action to a woman, and uses line-endings to subvert any obviously 'poetic' meter and push the rhythm towards a sense of the jagged asymmetry of actual speech:

Yes, love, that's why the warning light comes on. Don't
panic. Fetch some universal brake-fluid
and a five-eighths screwdriver from your toolkit
and prop the bonnet open. Go on, it won't

eat you.

But it is very clear that Armitage is deploying a range of poetic techniques in order to render the appearance of actual speech; in doing
so, moreover, he is in the company of a wide range of contemporary writers who have wanted to draw upon the resources of spoken language – as, for example, by using the mode of 'teenage *skaz*'
described by David Lodge. The 'magic realism' of novelists such as
Salman Rushdie and Angela Carter also depends crucially upon a
reference to orality, its self-consciously hybrid nature depends upon
the combining of textual and oral narrative techniques. This trend
is best understood by reference to the theorising about orality and
writing by Walter Ong, who describes the huge shift in human consciousness that takes place as a result of the shift from orality to
literacy. He lists the characteristics of oral cultures as they contrast
with textual cultures and shows how oral peoples believe that words,
and especially names, have magical power, and how the restriction
of words to sound 'determines not only modes of expression but also
thought processes'.[5] He then lists a series of nine characteristics of
oral expression and thought as they differ from textual expression
and thought. The first three of these are especially relevant to Simon Armitage, to teenage *skaz* and to magic realism; oral expression and thought is: '(i) Additive rather than subordinative' (p.37);
'(ii) Aggregative rather than analytic' (p.38) and '(iii) Redundant or
"copious"' (p.39).

In Armitage's version of oral forms like the joke, the anecdote,
the tall story and the public speech, these characteristics of orality
are fully exploited, as idiomatic sayings and clichés are relentlessly
piled on top of each other. So the speaker in 'Ivory' (*Zoom!*, p. 74)
undercuts himself by using too many words to demand an end to

mere chat:

> No more blab,
> none of that ragtag
>
> and bobtail business,
> or ballyhoo
> or balderdash
>
> and no jackassery, or flannel,
> or galumphing.

This is certainly additive, aggregative and copious, and the extent to which the effects of Armitage's early poems are linked to this is crucial because it is linked, also, to the questions which they self-reflexively raise about the subordinative and the analytic, about the authorial activity which would be required to organise material in that fashion. John Bayley's tone is sceptical when he describes the 'postmodernist trick of putting poetry . . . in inverted commas' – nonetheless it is a genuine achievement, in that it expresses urgent truths about contemporary experience. These poems achieve this by being, amongst other things, *about* the language of which they are composed, and they play with contemporary idioms to indicate how much experience is coloured, or even determined by them. But the self-consciousness of his deployment of these idioms is crucial: he does not use them simply to evoke an authentic voice. Instead that voice is treated with detachment that arises from the distance between the colloquial idioms and the poetic form in which they are placed, Armitage's stanzaic patterns. This introduces a poetic voice speaking alongside the colloquial one – a voice that seems simultaneously to be identified with, and sceptical of, the colloquial voice, and which simultaneously mocks its often trivial posturing and enjoys it.

The title sequence of Armitage's fourth book, *Book of Matches*, is organised around an oral performance. The first poem describes a 'party piece' which involves its speaker telling the story of his life in the length of time it takes a match to burn itself out. The distance between colloquial idiom and poetic form is again in evidence, because 'Book of Matches' is a sonnet sequence, but the sophisticated early modern courtly culture associated with that form is replaced by a contemporary, and at times only half-articulate, demotic idiom. Nor is this – as early modern sonnet sequences by Shakespeare and Sir Philip Sidney, for example, were – about love, and its lovelessness is part of its linguistic point, which focuses on mismatches. 'There are those who manage their private affairs/ and those who have to make a hash of theirs': these are the opening lines of a poem about a parachutist who is at odds even with himself:

Things he should want: safety first,
a perfect match, a straight indivisible two –
he wouldn't dream of leaping.
But he don't. So he do.

A safety match is a paradox which might have appealed to a contemporary Petrarch, given the Italian poet's love of oxymorons such as 'dolce nemica' (sweet enemy), or it might represent an impossible ideal of domestic passion to a modern Meredith, but the problem with this character is that what he should want and what he does want are mismatched. It is appropriate that it is not the parachutist himself who speaks the poem, but 'a friend of a friend' of his – we are at several unsympathetic removes from his state of mind, and the speaker suggests that it is lack of imagination, inability to dream of leaping, that makes him leap. Traditionally, poems should want experience and its expression also to be 'a straight indivisible two', but Armitage's sonneteering (like Paul Muldoon's) suggests formal desperation rather than form – his sonnets are broken, buckled, and ruinously lived in. There is a sadness, too, in the controlling metaphor that tends to make all the speakers seem like burnt-out cases, and to hint at a deathliness in the very process of structuring experience in language. The mauling that Armitage gives the sonnet sequence suggests profound mistrust of its suave symmetry, and the way that, through its complex and insistent rhyming, words and meanings, stories and lives, get persuasively matched.

One of the sonnets in this sequence deals with a medical condition called 'ankylosing spondylitis' (p. 21) and describes its symptoms as a problem with the bones causing them to stiffen and click. *Gig* refers to the condition as one which Armitage himself has suffered:

> When I was in my late twenties, and after a series of excruciating back problems that forced me to hang up my football boots and sell my stumping gloves, I was diagnosed as suffering from ankylosing spondylitis, a degenerative and at that time untreatable condition. I was told the vertebrae of my spine were slowly but surely knitting together, and that eventually I would develop a pronounced and painful hunch before seizing up altogether. (p.107)

Placing himself in the sequence, alongside the other speakers, and without privileging his voice at all, has the tendency – evident also elsewhere in his work – to estrange Armitage's own identity. His habit of referring to himself throughout *All Points North*, as in the sentence just quoted, as 'you', similarly hold his self at arm's length. He plays a connected trick elsewhere with references to his own name – 'Simon Says' (*Zoom!*, p. 40) and 'Armitage Shanks' (*The Universal Home Doctor*, p.20) – which insinuate his own ghostly presence in the poem. Self-estrangement is pushed further in Armitage's exploration of the notion of doubles. When he revisited Portsmouth University, where he was a student, to receive an honorary doctorate, he read out, at the degree ceremony, a poem in which he imagines a 'blank-faced kid', who is actually Armitage 'seen through two or three degrees of separation', who is 'looking up at himself through a twelve-year divide (*All Points North*, p. 199). Two poems that refer to the nineteenth-century poet Samuel Laycock, who grew up, like Armitage, in Marsden, and wrote poems in Lancashire dialect, refer to the idea of doubles across a class divide. 'To Poverty' (*Book* *ofMatches,*pp.38–9) addresses a 'shadow', a shapeless personage who lacks a face, and exhorts him ruefully to make himself at home in the speaker's house where the pair will live like 'sidekicks'. The speaker in 'The Two of Us' (*The Dead Sea Poems*, pp. 32–4) insists on a kinship between himself and a wealthy gentleman despite his own abject poverty, saying that his fellow villagers believe them to be alike, and have 'tapped me on the back and you've turned round'.

In 'All for One' (*The Universal Home Doctor*, pp.8–9) the speaker's mind detaches itself and lives a separate existence, though the speaker's complaint about this is not about that splitting of his self, but that his mind stalks him like a needy double, so that they are observed, from a distance, as identical shapes leading each other back into their house. That eerie image, and the context of self-estrangement that Armitage establishes, show his preoccupation with the alienness inside the self which has been a preoccupation ever since Freud theorised about the unconscious, and which has been evocatively described by Julia Kristeva:

> With Freud . . . foreignness, an uncanny one, creeps into the tranquillity of reason itself, and, without being restricted to madness, beauty, or faith any more than to ethnicity or race, irrigates our speaking-being, estranged by other logics, including the heterogeneity of biology . . . Henceforth, we know that we are foreigners to ourselves, and it is with the help of that sole support that we can attempt to live with others .[6]

In Armitage's 'Robinson' poems, which are parodies of Weldon Kees's poems which deal with his persona of the same name, Armitage explores the idea of authorial personae as uncanny doubles, and thereby suggests the relationship between those characters and their authors as an analogue for the elusiveness of the 'real' self. In 'Looking for Weldon Kees' (*Kid*, p.13) the search for the American poet (who mysteriously disappeared), and the way he gets confused with his persona, all question the extent to which the self, and especially other selves, are knowable. Nonetheless, there is a characteristic no-

nonsense approach by Armitage in this ontological exploration, and the Kees parodies are hardly even affectionate and sometimes mercilessly ridicule Kees's narcissistic *angst*, and imply that the Robinson persona barely functions as a Kees disguise, is largely an excuse for a displaced egotism, as in 'Mr.Robinson's Holiday' (pp.24–5) where the name is used twelve times ('Robinson thinking this is ridiculous, Robinson.')

Armitage repeatedly refers to people and characters who disappear. Kees is the most important because his vanishing is also an analogue for the disappearance of the author inside the text. But he has also has a character called Lucy, in his verse play Eclipse (*Cloud-CuckooLand*, pp.114–171), who disappears during a solar eclipse. And he has written about Albert Victor Grayson who 'shot to fame in a dramatic by-election in 1907 in Colne Valley – the first socialist ever to represent the constituency. He was dubbed as the greatest orator of his day, and tipped as a future leader of the Labour Party.' (*All Points North*, p. 158) But he was promiscuous and bisexual, liked to drink and party, lost his seat at the next election and failed to resurrect his career despite several attempts, and then, in 1920, he vanished:

> As a disappearing act, it made John Stonehouse's effort fifty-odd years later look like a game of hide and seek, and Grayson never returned from that place where Lord Lucan sits down to tea with Donald Crowhurst, and Elvis and Glenn Miller dream up a joint come-back album. (p. 159)

That catalogue of vanished celebrities, together with Armitage's concern with doubles, is linked to his preoccupation with an alienness inside the self. Taken together, these preoccupations indicate why the focus on authenticity and 'honesty' in Armitage's work is a simplification, as Armitage himself has said. In an early interview with Chris Greenhalgh, the interviewer says that Armitage's poems 'seem to *highlight* the elusiveness or relativity of truth' and Armitage replies:

I'm trying to think of a single instance when I've told some-thing 'straight' and I can't. I can't linger on the truth long enough to write about it, because eventually there will be an-other word or another phrase that comes to mind, and that's the one that I will want to use in the poem. I don't feel as if it's cheating, because it often helps to describe the sensa-tion I'm talking about, rather than saying 'That must be right, because that's what happened'. It occurs a lot at workshops where people argue 'But that's exactly how it happened', and I say 'Well, maybe, but it doesn't communicate to me as a piece of poetry, and if you want to describe that event you might have to talk about something completely different, you might have to be inventive, imaginative to relay that idea' and that's really what I try to do. I've done it in a lot of poems – got to a point where I've thought 'To express something here, I'll have to change tack and bring in another element' and at first I felt bad because I thought that I should use the truth as the script, but now it doesn't bother me at all.[7]

A case for postmodernist fictiveness in Armitage could be made on the basis of this statement, and with some justification. That would be less specific to Armitage, however, than showing how the elu-siveness of truth in his work is most often related to an ontological exploration, and the inaccessibility of the truth of the self. This is often turned upon the authorial self which is the central subject of the Robinson poems, where Armitage can be conveniently discussed in the context of postmodernist literature which metafictionally de-constructs the relationships between the author and the text, the author and the reader, and the reader and the text. A conspicuous example of such deconstruction is when novelists such as Paul Aus-ter and Martin Amis place characters with their own names in their novels. More distinctively Armitage's own, however, is a focus on that distance between selves which makes one person mysterious to another. It is this characteristic which Peter Sansom points out in 'Poem' (*Kid*, p.29) when he says that Armitage has chosen the title very much to point the relationship the poet (and reader) has with the character who 'exists' only in the textworld, a man who in a sense is merely a creation of the 'Poem'; and how in the end a person's life may mean just as little to his acquaintances; also, which attaches to Keats's notion of writing 'half at Random', how un-patterned, undesigned a life is: 'sometimes he did this, sometimes he did that'. [8]

The lack of design in the character's life could be considered a problem for a writer, and was certainly the kind of truth which struck modernist writers as an aesthetic problem – how do you make the connections that are required to make a work of art when life is disconnected and fragmentary? Armitage's statement of the point is particularly close to the language of modernist thinking in 'Sagitta' (*CloudCuckooLand*, p. 109) when he describes an attack in which a man was slashed across the face with a knife, and how the police said that the attack was not only motiveless, but had 'no meaning', so that the police are made to sound like modernist critics. It is another sign of the extent to which Armitage comes *after* modernism that 'Poem' treats the aesthetic problem with a shrug of the shoulders: Sansom is right to focus on the poem's form, and to indicate how its conspicuous patterns contrast with the stress on randomness in the biography. Instead of trying to iron out inconsistencies in the character, Armitage makes a poem out of framing them very rigidly in a sonnet with severely regular iambic pentameter. The shrug in the last line is the verdict of those who knew the man who is now evidently dead, how they 'rated' him, a word which implies an attempt to reach a moral appraisal which the conclusion then implies is impossible. That failure increases the distance between the man and those who knew him.

A poem from a decade later, 'The Shout' (*The Universal Home Doctor*, p. 3), is organised around an image that represents the distance between selves, as it remembers a schoolyard experiment aimed at working out how far the human voice can carry. One boy shouts and the other raises an arm if he can hear; the first boy moves progressively further away across a landscape that Armitage is very good at evoking as familiar. The shock comes with the sudden shift, in the last five lines, as twenty years have passed in which the shouting boy has emigrated to Australia and has been found with a bullet in his mouth. In his account of this poem in *Gig* (p.105), Armitage reveals that his ex-schoolmate shot himself – but as the speaker declares:

> Boy with the name and face I don't remember,
> you can stop shouting now, I can still hear you.

This theme in Armitage can be compared to a similar one in the poems of the Northern Irish poet Paul Muldoon who shares with the hero of his 'Why Brownlee Left' a profound restlessness expressed in his writing as self-conscious instability, a rejection of explanation and revelation, and a love of the unexplained and the unexplainable. In Muldoon's early work this takes the form of the question of the boundaries of personal identity; 'Identities', for example, describes a marriage of convenience which takes place because of external pressures and of mere chance, so that the fragility of selfhood is stressed. Muldoon's attempts to define personal identity lead to a preoccupation with origins and ancestry, but these provide no answer and lead to his obsession with hybridity, which, in terms of his poetic structures takes the form of dialogic mingling of discourses and registers. These ideas have been a key influence on Armitage; not all of them are necessarily attributable to influence from Muldoon because similar structures are evident in other poets – such as Craig Raine, Christopher Reid and James Fenton – of the previous generation to himself. As I have discussed elsewhere, [9] however, these forms are best understood by reference to the theories of Mikhail Bakhtin who describes the impact of 'novelisation' on poetry and for whom the exemplary figure was Dostoevsky who saw, he says many and varied things where others saw one and the same thing. Where others saw a single thought, he was able to find and feel out two thoughts, a bifurcation; where others saw a single quality, he discovered in it the presence of a second and contradictory quality . . . In every voice he could hear two contending voices, in every expression a crack, and the readiness to go over immediately to another contradictory expression; in every gesture he detected confidence and lack of confidence simultaneously; he perceived the profound ambiguity, even multiple ambiguity of every phenomenon. But none of these contradictions ever became dialectical, they were never set in motion along a temporal path or in an evolving sequence: they were, rather, spread out in one plane, as standing alongside or opposite one another, as consonant but not merging . . . as an eternal harmony of unmerged voices or as their unceasing and irreconcilable quarrel. Dostoevsky's visualising power was locked in place at the moment diversity revealed itself – and remained there, organizing and shaping this diversity in the cross section of a given moment. [10]

Simon Armitage is a conspicuously dialogic writer because he consistently evades simple lyric expression by his compulsion to 'change tack and bring in another element' which introduces what Bakhtin calls a 'bifurcation' in which diversity is revealed. He is so interested in narrative that he is happy to alter even his own story in order to tell it in a compelling way. And he restlessly switches from one literary form to another, so that, as well as poems, he has written songs, novels, plays, verse plays, scripts, journalism (especially music journalism), life writing, travel writing and nature writing – and he has also been willing to make references to all these forms and genres in his poems in order to find contending voices inside every voice, in order to open up a crack in any statement to stop it seeming monolithic. It is not surprising he has turned to the novel and to drama because his poems have always invented characters as their speakers, and have always questioned the generic authenticity of lyric or confessional poetry by mutating his own voice, and therefore his own identity inside the poem.

Dramatic monologue is the obvious genre in which such mutations occur, and Armitage has been as adept at writing in this form as his contemporary Carol Ann Duffy who is famous for her use of it. Despite its name, dramatic monologue is dialogic because it invents a character to speak the poem whose voice then interacts with the voice of the implied author. In Duffy's 'Psychopath', for example, the speaker is compared to a ventriloquist's dummy in order to indicate that the poet is speaking through him even as he speaks. The political point is clear and is connected to one of the major motives of Duffy's writing – to speak on behalf of those who are habitually spoken *for*. (As I will show later in this chapter, that motive has increasingly become Armitage's motive too.) Even a psychopath has aesthetic rights and deserves to be adequately represented: but that is achieved through the poem's self-reflexivity which owns up to the extent to which he is being caricatured. And that self-reflexivity is constructed most importantly through the strong sense of the dialogic which arises in 'Psychopath' because the presence of the poet's voice is strongly hinted at, especially in the context of Duffy's other poems which reveal her to be an intensely committed lesbian feminist. It is in the clash between that politically gendered perspective, and the perspective which will most horrify it – a serial killer of women – that the poem creates its vividly uncomfortable effects.

Robert Browning wrote the most famous early examples of dramatic monologue – 'My Last Duchess', 'Porphyria's Lover' – with murderers of women as their speakers. A murderer as a speaker is most able to display the impact of dramatic monologue in its contrast with lyric whose readers are called upon to recognise that they have experienced the same emotion as the author, called upon to understand and sympathise. When a speaker is explaining why he killed his victim, the point is that the reader is required to feel alienated and to refuse sympathy, and any sense that they have felt anything at all similar will be profoundly distressing. 'Gooseberry Season' (*Kid*, pp.1–2) is a matter-of-fact account – as these murder stories often are – of how the speaker and his family drowned a man in their bath and then dumped his body. The victim had lost his job and walked out of his house, leaving a note for his closest relatives, and so became another of Armitage's characters who go missing. The murderers let him live in their house but – like the tramp in Harold Pinter's *The Caretaker* – he outstays his welcome and starts to interfere in the family relationships. The juncture at which he oversteps the mark is measured by images which are characteristic of Armitage in being so thoroughly mundane that they read like colloquial idioms: the overstepped mark is as impossible to pinpoint as the place where the hand is now the wrist, or the neck is now the shoulder. The mundaneness, as always, is part of the point; here it adds plausibility to the representation of the speaker's voice, and it stresses the banality of evil. The most 'poetic' element in the poem is its eponymous image which arouses the speaker's memory because the victim had mentioned a recipe for gooseberry sorbet – the gooseberry season reminds him of the victim. The fact that he has to be reminded that he has murdered a house guest itself indicates his lack of feeling about the crime, but gooseberry sorbet confirms it in combining associations of what was once alive and fruitful and is now frozen. The victim has been 'iced', but his metonymic transformation into a dessert shows that the speaker regards the event as trivial.

The dialogic component of 'Hitcher' (*Book of Matches*, p. 46) is increased because, as well as containing the same implicit textual dispute between an affectless murderer and the implied author, it incorporates two other voices – the speaker's boss, whose warning on an ansaphone that he will sack the speaker if he hands in another sick note, is represented in italics, and the victim, whose conversation is reported by the speaker in free indirect speech. That also introduces a double voice, in this case resembling parody, as the monologuist paraphrases what the hitcher has said but in doing so mocks it. There is an implicit clash between the cultural perspective of the monologuist and that of the hitcher whose words, as dismissively reported by the speaker, are those of a hippy whose travelling is meant to be an expression of freedom and an organic relationship with the earth. The hippy is certainly made to sound annoying, and the reader of the poem (and possibly its addressee, because dramatic monologues are addressed, by implication, to someone listening) is called upon to be complicit with the killing of a victim who was so annoying that he deserved to die.

As Armitage's career develops, however, he becomes less interested in writing dramatic monologues spoken by obviously wrongheaded characters. There is still repeatedly the sense that the poems are not spoken unproblematically by the poet, but the moral status of what is said is rarely as simply wrong as it is in 'Gooseberry Season' and 'Hitcher'. The dialogic aspect of the poems gets increasingly focused on what Bakhtin calls 'heteroglossia', which involve the 'multiplicity' and the 'tendentious interaction' of different literary languages, and the way in which they derive from 'the stratification of social life, in which different social groups create distinctive discourses from their common language.'[11] So Armitage increasingly switches his interest from mimicking the voice of an individual speaker to mimicking the discourse of different linguistic communities, and this accompanies an increasingly explicit political attitude. Armitage's concern with class is notable here because class issues have tended to be relegated in importance in the postmodern (in late capitalism, with its emphasis on technology, the manifestations of class are less conspicuous than they were in high capitalism, with its heavy industry). Both *All Points North* and *Gig* – especially in their concern with the impact of Armitage's early formative experiences – take the interaction of region and class as motifs which give the books coherence. The two poems 'after Laycock', which I discussed earlier, and also 'The Laughing Stock' and 'The English' (*The Universal Home Doctor*, pp. 18–9 and 48) are all preoccupied with class – the latter with its gentleman farmer and its cricketer's widow living retrospective lives, and 'The Laughing Stock' with its dope-smoking, beer-drinking, channel-hopping, junk-food consuming, cash-strapped couch potatoes watching a TV program about the astonishingly alien lives of the aristocracy.

But Armitage's political preoccupations stretch beyond class into a more general indictment of the injustices perpetrated by governments and by global capitalism; I discuss Armitage's developing ecological anxieties in my chapter on his 'Changes of Place'. The poem that starts *Tyrannosaurus Rex versus the Corduroy Kid* is his most obviously polemical verse, in its attack on the treatment of Dr. David Kelly by the Blair administration, and takes the phrase 'washing your hands of a problem' and makes it literal as a set of 'government guidelines'. The object of the satire here is also the patronising advice repeatedly issued by recent governments about matters of personal health and hygiene, so that the mingling of this register with the government's unconcern about Kelly's health works by the dialogic attention it draws to this 'tendentious interaction'. The poem is instructive, therefore, in drawing attention to the broadly political impact of Armitage's wide-ranging embrace of heteroglossia as an indicator of the complex interplay of different forces within contemporary society. These heteroglossia include his references to Biblical and apocalyptic language in *The Dead Sea Poems*; the metaphoric uses of astronomy in *CloudCuckooLand*; the contrasts between the domestic (and notions of a 'homeland') and the exotic in *The Universal Home Doctor*; and his references to a diverse set of 'natural' languages (nature writing, ecopoetry) in *Tyrannosaurus Rex versus the Corduroy Kid*. His 2010 book *Seeing Stars* adopts, throughout, a playful ironic mode akin to that of poets influenced by John Ashbery but who are less committed to Derridean scepticism than Ashbery – poets such as the British poet John Ash and the Americans Frederick Seidel and August Kleinzaler.

Alongside all this, however, there has been an opposite trend in other aspects of Armitage's work, towards what might be called an anti-dialogic agenda – a determination to speak straightly, directly and honestly – which is connected to the growing urgency of his political concerns. It is worth looking again at his Greenhalgh interview when he says 'at first I felt bad because I thought that I should use the truth as the script, but now it doesn't bother me at all.' That he felt bad at first is telling because it is certain that thorough postmodernists would not have felt any guilt on this score at all. Since he made that remark he first of all developed further in the dialogic direction, but then started to turn against it and make determined efforts to 'use the truth as the script'. Armitage's development can be gauged in the differences between two poems which look superficially similar, 'Ivory' and 'D-notice', the first from *Zoom!* (p. 74), and the second from *The Dead Sea Poems* (pp. 30–1). The earlier poem enjoys the joke of a Pinteresque flood of language which demands silence: the later one uses the same joke but in a political context which makes the demand much more threatening, and the verbs to 'tie' and to 'clamp' suggest the violence of censorship and suppression.

The new directness is connected, in particular, to the films Armitage has made with Brian Hill, – the earliest of which, 'Saturday Night' (whose script appears in *All Points North*), dates from 1996. In *Gig* he describes his role as songwriter on a project ten years later, where the film was called *Songbirds* and was set in Downview Prison in Surrey, and was a sequel to *Feltham Sings* which was made in Feltham Young Offenders' Institution. In both films the prisoners 'talk about their experiences of offending and prison life, then suddenly burst into song.' (p. 52) Armitage only visited the prison once:

I then sat at home, 200 miles away, with a minidisc player in one hand and a pen in the other, listening to the spoken testimonies of several prisoners and trying to turn them into lyrics. I could have spent more time in the prison, but I don't think it would have helped. I'm the sort of writer who needs distance and dispassion to be able to tackle a subject. For me, writing is like dissecting a rat – something done with a clinical eye under laboratory-type conditions. To get more involved on a personal level might have meant donning my probation officer's hat again, when the poet's one has become so comfortable. I've already given up the job once – I don't want to go back. (p.53)

This activity provides the key to what was involved for Armitage in providing the script for his poem-films, where the major effort is to be as authentic as possible while still drawing upon the resources of poetry to the extent that they can work alongside film. It is important that Armitage is transmitting the experience of real people and that he retains in his poetic versions a genuine sense of who they are and what they felt. An analogy would be with First World War poetry where a crucial part of the impact is that the poets are describing what they themselves have directly experienced, except in Armitage's case the real experience is at one remove and is recaptured through a strenuous act of imaginative sympathy. Armitage refers to the First World War poets in relation to the film *The Not Dead* : in his 'Introduction' to that he describes those poets 'sending back first-hand literary reports' (p. x) and that is the effort he imitates in his poem-films. So for *The Not Dead* he visited war veterans and then translated their accounts into poems. While these writings lack the rich dialogic complexity of his other work, they need to be seen as operating in a different generic area where the words are very effective in combination with the pictures which they were designed to accompany. The obvious analogy is with song-writing: and certainly in films like *The Not Dead* the end product is impressive and moving.

Notes

1. Philip Gross, 'Slangland', *Poetry Review*, Summer 1992, p.56.

2. Graham Mort, 'The Guy from Marsden', *Poetry Review*, Spring 1990, p. 64.

3. David Lodge, *The Art of Fiction*, (Harmondsworth: Penguin, 1992) p. 18.

4. John Bayley, *Poetry Review*, Summer 1993, p.15.

5. Walter Ong, *Orality and Literacy* (London: Routledge, 1988) p. 33.

6. Julia Kristeva, *Strangers to Ourselves*, trans. L.S.Roudiez, (London, Harvester Wheatsheaf, 1994) p.170.

7. Chris Greenhalgh, 'Simon Armitage: An Interview with Chris Greenhalgh', *Bete Noire*, Autumn 1991/Spring 1992, p. 271.

8. Peter Sansom, 'Reading for Writing: Simon Armitage' in Lesley Jeffries and Peter Sansom eds., *Contemporary Poems: Some Critical Approaches* (Huddersfield,Smith/Doorstop Books, 2000)p.88.

9. Ian Gregson, *Contemporary Poetry and Postmodernism: Dialogue and Estrangement* (Basingstoke: Macmillan, 1996).

10. M.M.Bakhtin, *The Dialogic Imagination: Four Essays by M.M.Bakhtin*, trans. Caryl Emerson and Michael Holquist (Austin: University of Texas Press, 1981), p.7.

11. Nancy Glazener, 'Dialogic Subversion: Bakhtin, the novel and Gertrude Stein' in Ken Hirschkop and David Shepherd, eds., *Bakhtin and Cultural Theory* (Manchester: Manchester University Press, 1989) p. 109.

3

ARMITAGE: MAN AND BOY

Simon Armitage's TV script 'Jerusalem' (*All Points North*, pp. 124–48) is centred upon the rivalry between two powerful men. JE (John Edward Castle) 'enjoys power and influence, both in his own home and in the town' and was formerly 'station-master in the local fire service, but an accident at work left him incapacitated and housebound'(p. 126). Spoon was formerly the police inspector, a 'hard man' – so hard that he rescued JE from a fire while 'the fire brigade looked on in oxygen masks and steamed-up goggles' (p.128) – but then softened enough to fall in love with JE's wife, Rose, when he met her in the hospital when he visited JE. The comic exaggeration in these portraits makes even starker their focus upon the masculinity of the two rivals who 'detest each other' (p.128) and their relentless belligerence contrasts with Rose's function of managing an 'unsteady truce' in the household where she is 'wife, nursemaid and housekeeper' (p. 130). JE's power is both domestic and political, but his disability has reduced his macho status by rendering him 'housebound', so confining him to a setting associated with women, and making 'communication' become 'central to [his] regime', when masculinity ought to be most thoroughly expressed through action. He must now rely on his sidekick, whose name 'Softie' indicates his own inferior gender status by stressing his lack of the requisite hardness – he is 'subordinate and obedient' (p. 131) – but it also indicates the diminishment which his master, JE, has suffered. By contrast

Spoon is 'six-foot odd and powerfully built', 'always well turned out', and he is 'forceful and persuasive, always one step ahead, never appearing ruffled or wrong-footed' (p. 129). The thorough completeness of his masculine identity is confirmed by Rose's continuing love for him, and the fact that he is the real father of Wesley Castle who he comes to influence when they regularly meet to fish (p.136). Wesley's own masculinity, however, is constantly undermined: persuaded by his father to become a volunteer fireman, he becomes terrified when he has to enter a burning farmhouse and wets himself and has to be rescued (p.145). JE is appalled to discover that Wesley is reading a book called *Pump or Penis? Feminist Interpretations of FireFighting*.

That joke indicates that Armitage's gender awareness has been influenced by feminism; growing up in the 1960s and 70s meant that he was shaped by a cultural context in which gender assumptions were being increasingly deconstructed. The impact of feminism on male poets can be measured by the differing attitudes of those, like Seamus Heaney, who grew up before feminism was influential, and those, like Paul Muldoon, young enough to have absorbed its effect on the attitudes of men and women. Heaney consistently feminises the Irish landscape; he describes himself as 'betrothed' to 'green, wet corners, flooded wastes, soft rushy bottoms'; discussing Patrick Kavanagh he is taken with the 'notion that the curve of the hill is the curve of a loved one's beauty, its contour the contour of a woman with child'.[1] This means that digging and ploughing are regarded as masculine acts performed upon the passive body of the earth. Heaney considers his poem 'Digging' a rite of passage poem through which he ceased to be 'Incertus', it was an initiation into the poeticosexual act, in which 'digging becomes a sexual metaphor, an emblem of initiation' (*Preoccupations*, p.42). From the start of his career – as I have argued elsewhere[2] – Heaney endows the poetic act with associations of male sexuality and power in which the two are thoroughly mingled, and charges these associations with spiritual meaning. He defines the masculine and feminine as rigid polarities and then imposes them systematically as such on his subject-matter: in other words he expresses precisely those gender attitudes which feminism has been most concerned to deconstruct, his attitudes are 'essentialist' in that they assume that men and women have essential differences arising from hormones and instincts.

By contrast Paul Muldoon rejects such essentialism, especially in his treatment of father figures as problematic models of masculinity and questionable sources of original truth, and for him the key metaphor is the hybrid, an image which opposes Heaney's metaphor of the poem as male heir (see, for example, 'Follower') with an emphasis on the bastard mingling of textual materials, on subversive miscegenation. Muldoon's 'Mules' is concerned, not just with a biological metaphor for a hybrid of earth and heaven, which are combined in the sexual act which is the central event in the poem, but with the way that languages and perspectives mingle, and, in a sense, reproduce. The numerous references in Muldoon's poems to his father, and his concern with the epic theme of the search for the lost father – especially in 'Immram' – suggest that there is something self-reflexive in this also, that the poem is created in the process of recreating the figure who created the poet. Stated like this the theme might sound po-faced and masculinist, but it is treated with characteristic irony by Muldoon, and in such playful and fictive ways, that the search for authenticity, or male 'authority', which it implies, is self-consciously subverted.

Simon Armitage has referred to one of his earliest poems, 'Greenhouse', as dedicated to his father, and Peter Sansom, having quoted that remark, notes how the poem deals with 'something abstract – the relationship between father and son – through description.'[3] However, it also deals with that abstraction intertextually by its careful reference, in its description of how father and son built the greenhouse, to the son following the father:

I remember that journey:
you out in front, unsure of your footing
on the damp stones, and me behind counting
each of your steps through our cargo of glass. (*Zoom!*, p.13)

That image of the son behind the father who is, by implication, in charge at first and expert at what he is doing, appears at the end of the first stanza, and then again in the last line, with the poet 'just one step behind', and it is vividly reminiscent of Seamus Heaney's 'Follower', in which Heaney's father is depicted as the complete master of the craft of ploughing, and the young Heaney as walking constantly behind him, ambitious to acquire that mastery but instead being merely an over-talkative nuisance. In the last two lines of Heaney's poem, however, the hierarchy has been reversed; it is now the son who is the expert, as the poem's suave technique demonstrates, and the father who has declined, and who stumbles, rather pathetically, behind the son. The symmetry in the idea of following defines the role reversal and is chilling, it seems heartlessly dismissive of the father's loss of potency and exults in how that decline makes the son's rise all the more conspicuous. At the same time, however, the last lines hint at guilt on the son's part about his feelings of having triumphed over his father, anxious identification with his father's vulnerability, and sadness at his decline. Paul Muldoon has repeatedly referenced and parodied 'Follower', and in 'Greenhouse' Armitage adds his own response to the intertextual dialogue. As Sansom says:

> 'gone to seed' means ceasing to flower as the seed begins to grow, and it describes the father as the son comes into his own, begins as it were to blossom. It's a loving poem, but it's clear-eyed about this. Or maybe we feel the greenhouse represents only the relationship, that the days of the son as a sort of apprentice are numbered and that father and son are simply becoming equals. Except there are the final words of the poem ... Literal, again, this description, but the figurative is close to the surface, insisted on in fact or why else have both 'you, out in front' and 'me behind ...'? We see the 'footing' they're on, the father unsteady, the son confident (trusting?) enough not to look at his own feet but to watch his father's instead, to keep the rhythm of their progress. (p. 80)

Sansom is characteristically acute on the emotional meaning of the poem's images, but 'Greenhouse' can only be understood fully if his insights are also placed in their intertextual context: a major part of the answer to his question 'why else have both?' is to emphasise that the relative positions of father and son, and their figurative significance, mirror that in the Heaney poem. In fact I would say that the full implications of 'Greenhouse', and its relationship to Armitage's other poems, can only be understood if their gender context is described – and that is my intention in this chapter. Most pressingly relevant here, for Heaney and Muldoon as well as for Armitage, is that there have been a remarkably large number of Anglophone poems published in the postwar era, many of them famous, on the subject of father-son relationships – far more than were published in earlier periods. This in itself suggests increased gender awareness on the part of male poets. In *Life Studies*, Robert Lowell repudiates his father who he regards as savourless and unmasterful in favour of his grandfather, his mother's father, who embodies all the frontier values which he regards as truly masculine. The ambivalence in his retrospective account of how he learned masculinity from those grandfatherly values insists on how much gender insecurity lies behind it and how comically, mock-heroically inappropriate this version of manliness appears for contemporary males. John Berryman's *Dream Songs* continually grieves over a loss which is related, implicitly or explicitly, to the suicide of Berryman's father: this loss always seems to lie behind any other which he mentions, forming for him the paradigm of loss. His emotional responses to the suicide vary – from grieving to sympathy to moral disapproval to the anger of 384, the penultimate Dream Song, where Berryman imagines himself spitting on his father's grave. Ted Hughes wrote three poems about his father, 'Out', 'Dust as we Are' and 'For the Duration', and they all focus on his father's war experiences and their impact on the Hughes household, especially on the poet himself. Hughes senior is shown in the process of recuperating, but Hughes junior is learning what it is to be a man through identifying with his father's suffering as a soldier. The damage he suffered is accounted for partly in Blakeian terms; it is caused by powerful feelings which mangled him because they were not allowed free expression. The consequences of the damage, though, are referred to a Wordsworthian model in their effect on the growth of the poet's soul – the Hughes organism grows, but in a diseased form.

If the father poems by Heaney and Muldoon are added to this list, a formidable picture emerges of the most important heterosexual male poets in the postwar period dwelling on the psychological importance of their interactions with their fathers. It is not an accident, then, that Simon Armitage has placed a poem early in his first book that positions him in relation to this tradition, that shows him following in the footsteps of his poetic forefathers as well as those of his actual father. But whereas the mature Heaney only followed his father metaphorically by making ploughing an analogy for writing a poem, Armitage literally followed his father by becoming a probation officer:

I was a probation officer and my father was a probation officer before me. Not exactly the family business; more a case of him paving the way and me following in his footsteps. He did his training at Manchester University and twenty years later so did I. I was interviewed by the same man, very probably in the same office, very possibly sitting in the same chair. During my interview I talked seamlessly and with great conviction about public attitudes to offending, about recent legislation in the criminal justice system, about social policy and the welfare state, and about the role of the caring professions in advanced capitalist societies. After about half an hour the man taking notes leaned back in his swivel chair, put his hands behind his head and his feet on the bookshelf and said, 'OK, OK. Anyway, how's your dad?' (*Gig*, p.289)

What distinguishes Armitage from his major predecessors, however, is his increased gender self-consciousness, so that he is thoroughly aware not just of the implications of his relationship with his father, but of how that relationship should be regarded in the wider context of gender interactions and attitudes in what he refers to here as 'advanced capitalist societies'. In 'Jerusalem' he represents his own generation in Wesley and dwells on the character's awareness of gender questions, which is more acute because Wesley is the focus of anxieties about manliness. This point is even more pressing in the final incarnation of *Jerusalem* as a stage play, in which Softie's role as unmanly sidekick is taken over by Wesley as he bribes the natives of the village to vote for his father for the role of Entertainments secretary. Wesley refers to the fire brigade (in the phrase Armitage avoids using about the probation service) as the 'family business' (p. 16) so that his failure at it represents his failure to acquire adult masculinity as it is understood by his elders, and his failure is emphasised when one of the firemen says 'Wesley, do the washing-up, love, there's a good chap. Plenty of *Fairy* – keep those hands nice and soft. ' (p.16) The accusation that Wesley is gay is repeated by both JE and by Wesley's grandmother (pp. 35, 37), though it is only Wesley himself who makes the accusation completely explicit: 'what will they be saying? That John Edward Castle fathered a queer – is that what you're worried about?' (p. 37)

The accusation is important, not just in the routine homophobia which it satirises, but, also, in what it represents in terms of what is required of men if they are to be regarded as fully masculine. As Judith Butler has pointed out:

Although Freud introduces the Oedipal complex to explain why the boy must repudiate the mother and adopt an ambivalent attitude towards the father, he remarks shortly afterward that 'It may even be that the ambivalence displayed in the relations to the parents should be attributed entirely to bisexuality and that it is not, as I have represented above, developed out of identification in consequence of rivalry.' But what would condition the ambivalence in such a case? Clearly, Freud means to suggest that the boy must choose not only between the two object choices, but the two sexual dispositions, masculine and feminine. That the boy usually chooses the heterosexual would, then, be the result, not of the fear of castration by the father, but of the fear of castration – that is, the fear of 'feminization' associated within heterosexual cultures with male homosexuality. [4]

The gay smears levelled at Wesley do not primarily imply that he is attracted to men. They refer to his lack of the active masculinity that would drive him to take initiatives and acquire a girlfriend (JE's accusation that Wesley lies in bed and pulls his pudding (p. 30) is a related insult) and they refer to his 'softness', his lack of phallic determination.

The fire brigade, like the probation service, is the Armitage family business because Armitage's father is also an 'ex-fireman' (*Gig*, p. 152). The accusations of gayness are also ones which Armitage recounts his father making against him – if only as taunts relating to the unmanly personal style of the younger generation. In his New Romantic phase, Armitage had his ear pierced, but his father avoided direct confrontation and plotted a different revenge:

> A couple of days later when I walked into the club I was met with wolf-whistles, limp-wristed hand gestures and a beery chorus of 'All the Nice Boys Love a Sailor'. Dad just shrugged his shoulders and raised his drink to his mouth, as if suggesting the local tribe's reaction to my act of self-mutilation was entirely spontaneous and beyond his control. (*Gig*, p.8)

A version of this story is given to one of the speakers in *Book of Matches* (p.12), but in this case the father speaks directly and calls the earring 'bloody queer'. The speaker rebukes himself at the end of the poem, and is surprised to hear his voice 'breaking like a tear', where 'breaking' can refer to the male adolescent change of voice, as well as to fragmentation, which is repeated in the secondary meaning of 'tear'. So the father's accusation of queerness leads to the speaker doubting the fullness of his own masculine maturity with the suspi-

cion that he is breaking down like a boy (or even a girl), and resolves
to rid himself of the earring.

On another occasion when Armitage walked through the living
room with a copy of *Ziggy Stardust*, his father said 'David Bowie? He's
a homosexual.' (*Gig*, p.202) and banned his music from their house.
These stories draw attention to the different gender attitudes of the
two generations and indicate that Armitage's outlook was influenced at an early age by a popular culture which was questioning
conventional rigidities: in the first decade of Armitage's life, Bowie
was experimenting with the science-fiction gender-bending of the
Ziggy persona and declaring himself to be bisexual. *Jerusalem* makes
one explicit reference to Bowie's earlier character Major Tom (p. 41)
but makes another, more implicit, to the idea of an astronaut float-
ing in a tin can when it wants to evoke ideas of heroic, but solipsis-
tic, masculinity in relation to Spoon (p.31); Armitage's account of
the movement from Major Tom to Ziggy as 'a bisexual alien with a
buzz-saw guitar' reveals a sense that the movement towards gender
ambiguity represents an increase in hip awareness. His description
of Bowie's career associates the questioning of gender roles with a
charismatically progressive attitude, 'the look and feel of something
new' (*Gig*, p. 201).

JE accuses Rose of molly-coddling Wesley and thereby com-
promising his growth into manliness, but Wesley is no more gay
than Armitage is, and the play makes Wesley represent a version
of straight masculinity that is different from that expected by JE –
more sensitive and intelligent, more like water than fire (Wesley's
day job is with the Water Board, and his hobby is fishing). Wesley
does finally acquire the girlfriend that his grandmother and JE demand he must have, but he does so through the woman's initiative,
and comic insistence, and not through his own actions (in fact he
fails even to notice her initiative at first). Before that, though, he has
a conversation with Spoon in which he makes a comment which is
the most remarkable gender moment in Armitage's canon. Wesley
is expounding on the psychological meaning of fishing and says that
Freud interprets it in terms of

fluidity and so on. It's maternal, of course. The subconscious, the transforming ocean, the boundless sea. And the womb, obviously, the intrauterine birth and the breaking of the water. (p.39)

Wesley's male feminist analysis reveals the extent of Armitage's gender awareness and gives the lie to critics like James Wood who underestimate that awareness: lamenting Armitage's influence on Don Paterson he says that the Scottish poet 'needs to avoid the blokeish bluntness of Simon Armitage'. [5] In fact Armitage has deliberately evolved a masculine style in which blokeishness is deconstructed with a sharp self-consciousness. Wesley's comment is reminiscent of the evocations of the ocean in the writings of the post-Lacanian French feminist Luce Irigaray, who simultaneously celebrates the ocean and indicts a masculinity which hardens its heart to 'the glorious assault of her colours, to the fascination of her sheer size, to the seduction of her smells and sounds'. [6]

Wesley goes on to reference the symbolic antitheses, as defined by Jung, of water (his own element) and fire, which is 'consuming and destructive and masculine' (p.39). In those terms, Armitage's own element is definitely fire – as his long poem 'Five Eleven Ninety Nine' (*The Dead Sea Poems*, pp. 36–57) proves with its painstakingly extended description of the building of a November the 5th bonfire which brilliantly acquires a range of symbolic meanings focused on the ideas of apocalypse and renewal. The poem lingers with evident fascination over its lengthy listing of a diverse range of wooden materials and their diverse origins, and then over their gradual assembling into the correct structure for the bonfire, via preliminary shapes which are successively superceded, and over the addition of materials which will aid combustion, such as coal, petrol and kerosene, and then over the applying of the match, and the first failed attempts, and then over the gradual growth of the flame, with an especially evocative reference to the appearance of 'a chamber' inside the structure, an interior which is alight, and then the spreading outwards into a growing conflagration. Armitage's own account of his motives for writing 'Five Eleven Ninety Nine' also confirms the point:

> when I was younger, I promised myself that I'd write a book about bonfires, believing myself a world expert in their construction and the art of lighting them. As a kid, 5 November rated alongside birthdays and Christmas, although the last bonfire I took any active part in ended in tears, when a five-inch nail went through my boot and straight through my foot as well. I watched the blaze from my bedroom window, lapped in bandages, coming to terms with it.[7]

Armitage, therefore, has the opposite gender sensibility to Wesley, and is drawn to the 'consuming and destructive and masculine' element. So far, at least, – and it must be constantly stressed that Armitage is still only half-way, at most, through his career – he has never paid anything like a similar tribute to water as the one he pays to fire in 'Five Eleven Ninety Nine'. He still has plenty of time to make the sort of change which Robert Lowell made when he developed away from the discomfort and inhibition in the face of the sea he expressed in 'The Quaker Graveyard in Nantucket', which is about agonized attempts to impose dominion over the ocean, through the attempt in 'Near the Ocean' to accommodate the ocean-as-mother only guiltily and up to a point. In his later work Lowell allows freer play to the oceanic imaginary, and, through the linked figures of the mermaid and the dolphin, learns not to harden his heart to the sea, and, thereby, to allow a new accommodation of the feminine. Meanwhile, Armitage's element is definitely fire, and the key point for his writing is his precise knowledge of that fact, and it is one of the most striking features of his work that he has an intensely masculine sensibility but is also intensely aware of it. That is a very rare combination because it has always previously been a characteristic of thorough masculinity that it should not reflect on itself as such. Partly this may be because three of Armitage's avowed influences – as I discuss in my chapter on his contexts – W.H. Auden, Thom Gunn and Frank O'Hara – were gay, while two others, Ted Hughes and Robert Lowell, were decidedly heterosexual and even macho.

So Armitage's writing has contributed to a contemporary deconstruction of gender, especially in its concern with the ways that men respond to the demand to aquire a masculine identity as it has traditionally been understood. Seen from this perspective, the title poem of *Kid* can be placed in the same context as 'Greenhouse', as dealing with the need of the young male to assert his mature identity in the face of the challenge represented by the older figure of paternal authority. It is characteristic of Armitage's fondness for comic and ironic modes, and for parody, that the poem is spoken by a comic-strip character, but the caricatural mode is just as telling here – as it is in *Jerusalem* – when Robin asserts his own masculinity against that of Batman, proclaiming that he is now 'taller, harder, stronger, older', proclaiming that 'now I'm the real boy wonder'. (*Kid*, p.36) David T. Evans has characterised the 'ideal masculine qualities' as those of 'dominance, activity, autonomy, impersonality and rationality'. This traditional male role involves, he says:

> 'no sissy stuff' – the avoidance of all feminine behaviours and
>   traits:
> 'the big wheel' – the acquisition of success, status, and bread-
>   winning competence:
> 'the sturdy oak' – strength, confidence and independence:
> 'give 'em hell' – aggression, violence and daring. [8]

The prohibition of sissiness, of earrings in the case of Armitage, and of watery cowardice in the case of Wesley, is the prerequisite for success and status, which will then allow the younger male to supercede the older. Batman was a 'big shot' who ordered Robin to grow up and then forced him out into the world: his comeuppance is achieved because Robin has followed his order literally to the extent that he can now become his own man, and Batman is left doing his own domestic chores and is even addressed by Robin as 'baby'.

This confrontation is characteristic because Armitage likes to express these themes through competitiveness. His first novel *Little Green Man* is driven by that theme as a group of reunited old school-friends, all male, set each other increasingly disturbing challenges to win the eponymous statuette whose ownership, in their child-hood, determined who would be the leader of their gang. Sport fea-tures repeatedly in the novel and Armitage often draws upon athlet-ic games – especially football and cricket – as analogies, while (again characteristically) refreshing the clichéd aspects of such analogies. By his own account, the focus of his interest is in the need to over-come obstacles and is derived from his own struggle with spondili-tis, which I discuss in the chapter 'Armitage's Voices'. He connects that struggle to his poem 'The Winner' (*CloudCuckooLand*, p. 7), which describes 'a person whose bodily malfunctions have reached ludi-crous proportions, but despite losing almost every limb and func-tion . . . manages to take the life-saving test at his local swimming baths and complete the Lyke Wake Walk.' (*Gig*, p. 108) Armitage does not draw attention, here, though, to the poem's mode of uncomfort-able black comedy, resembling gallows humour, or, more relevant-ly, the humour shared by soldiers and other males in dire straits – whereas in *All Points North* (p. 81) he does so by relating the poem to a joke his father used to tell about a man who has, in turn, both his arms and then a leg amputated and asks, each time, if the limb can be returned to England to be buried. But when he has his other leg amputated the authorities refuse permission saying ' "We think you're trying to escape." '

The catalogue of catastrophic ailments is matched by the corre-sponding catalogue of grotesque prostheses which are given their victim as solutions to the continuing disappearance of bits of his body, so that he turns into a sort of wonky cyborg. But this is one of those poems with a 'volta' that divides it into two: sonnets have that division built into their form, and 'The Winner', though longer, de-scribes terrible losses, and the implication that the victim is a loser, in its first verse paragraph, and then describes his triumphs over these adversities in its second. Despite everything, the 'winner' be-comes a 'big wheel' and exhorts his parents to be proud of him, tells his mother to cherish the badge he won for completing the walk, and tells his father to picture his son completing the life-saving test. The imagery that accompanies those exhortations is of a hard masculinity – his nerves are 'steel', his will is 'iron', his heart is a 'waterpump' and his chest is a 'battleship': against the odds, he has become a 'sturdy oak'. So the pattern which the poem's volta follows is similar (especially if it is related to the joke of Armitage senior about the wartime amputee) to that which Ted Hughes follows when he repeatedly expresses the fear that the self is scattered in pieces, but that there is the hope of a new wholeness resembling rebirth. Later in his work he links this preoccupation with archetypal patterns discernible in Egyptian mythology, as Keith Sagar points out when he refers to 'the reassembling of the bits and pieces of disintegrated man', which occurs so often in Hughes's poems, as 'a version of the Osiris story.'[9] In *The Iron Man* – possibly Hughes's most famous publication – the hero is pictured at the start falling apart and all his pieces tumbling down a cliff onto the beach below. Then, bit by bit, he puts himself together again all except for one ear which has been taken by a gull and lies on a ledge of the cliff. Like Hughes's Iron Man, and like his thrushes which resemble 'coiled steel',[10] and his roosting hawk, Armitage's 'winner' represents an aspiration towards a supercharged and entirely secure masculinity characterised by iron hardness and unwavering unstoppable activity. To use the terms adopted by one of the best theorists of masculinity, Lynn Segal, these figures represent an attempt to replace the fragility of the penis with the invulnerability of the phallus:

Masculinity is never the undivided, seamless construction it becomes in its symbolic manifestation. The promise of phallic power is precisely this guarantee of total inner coherence, of an unbroken and unbreakable, an unquestioned and unquestionable masculinity. Deprived of it, how can men be assured of 'natural' dominance? The antagonisms of gender coalesce with the strains of affirming and maintaining sexual polarities.[11]

Armitage's major difference from Hughes on these subjects, however, is his knowingness, which means that he draws upon these
images but at the same time ironises them and makes them half-
comic. As Sarah Broom has written, 'Despite the consistently masculine viewpoint in Armitage's poems, we are prevented from laps-
ing into a state of inattentiveness regarding gender by Armitage's
fascination with the contours and contradictions of masculinity.' [12]
Dennis O'Driscoll notes that 'Armitage has described "Goalkeeper
with a Cigarette", his hymn to nonchalance, as a "manifesto" ', [13] and
that poem clearly represents for him the ideal style, the one to aim
for when the struggle in 'The Winner' has been won, though it is
'The Winner' which he twice describes as featuring conspicuously in
his readings. The point of 'Goalkeeper with a Cigarette' (*The Dead Sea
Poems*, pp.16–7) is to imagine a level of talent which transcends the
need to struggle, and is so at home with itself that it eschews display
in favour of understated and thoroughly relaxed brilliance. But the
goal in which he is custodian is very much a goal to strive for, rather
than one that is readily available, and the obvious realist point that
no world-class goalkeepers smoke during games is worth making
because it reinforces the fantasy element which is dominant – as,
also, does the third-person narration which contrasts with the first-
person mode of 'The Winner', where the sense of identification is
much more intense. The goalkeeper personifies phallic power, the
repeated 'That's him', and the dwelling on the word 'man', and the
declaration 'He is what he is' all emphasise his 'total inner coherence' and his 'unbroken and unbreakable' masculinity. A related
fantasy is in 'Great Sporting Moments: The Treble' (Kid, p.55) where
class revenge is inflicted firstly in tennis (with shots that resemble
a train and a rubber bullet) and then at golf: the first is achieved
through expertise gained on the impoverished courts of West Yorkshire, the second by a faux naiveté made believable by his accent.
The poem's title indicates that the speaker is destined to win the
third contest proposed by his rich opponent who, in frustration, demands a boxing match. His reply, in the last line, with its seven con-

secutive 'noes' which issue into his apparently reluctant acceptance, is Armitage's most famous piece of dialogue.

However much these masculine fantasies are enjoyed by Armitage, his gender self-consciousness has led him increasingly to indict the damage caused by masculinity in its most untrammelled forms. Some of his most memorable poems concern the emotional unresponsiveness, or inflexibility, or muteness of men. Sean O'Brien relates these moments to a regional consciousness:

> It is a vague formulation: but there is something I recognise as Northern about Armitage – a guarded flatness and watchfulness that oversee even his most zestful work and make his best poems, which are mainly about love, seem like exceptions to a general rule of sensibility. Paradoxically, even his garrulity is somehow close-mouthed, as if meant to be accessible to a group rather than the generality. [14]

There is some truth in this, and O'Brien describes this aspect of Armitage extremely well, and his point is to some extent confirmed by the way it can be related to another connection with Ted Hughes whose horrified description of his father's influence dwells on his refusal actually to talk about the First World War trauma he was suffering. Hughes's 'Dust As We Are' refers to war as a guilty secret which men keep from women, and 'For the Duration' describes his father as so silent that he appears to be listening on a telephone, while the poet eavesdrops on the line. So Hughes describes his four-year-old self being burdened with feelings precisely because those feelings remain unexpressed, and giving draining emotional support to a father who is unable to give it back. 'Out' declares that the buffeting which his father's body has received has made it 'wordless' so that it is only the maleness of that body that allows the son to identify with the father and to learn at the same time that males are warriors who do not speak about what they do or feel. While it is true that Hughes and Armitage are connected through regional experience as poets from Yorkshire, the more important connection

here is their shared preoccupation with masculine experience, and
the inability to discuss it – in this case war. In 2008 Armitage published the poems he wrote for a Channel 4 film called *The Not Dead*
in which he versified the accounts of war experiences recounted to
him by veterans:

> Cliff's feelings of guilt and shame have only increased with
> age and the pictures in his head are as clear today as they were
> half a century ago. At 75 he can't talk about the jungle ambush
> he was involved in without tears rolling down his face, and
> when it comes to speaking of his fellow soldiers who died in
> the attack, he can barely get the words out of his mouth. (p.xii)

Cliff is a victim of the same kind of war trauma which afflicted Ted
Hughes's father, and in versifying it Armitage is attempting to over-
come that inhibition about expressing the trauma which has such
a representative significance for masculine identity. Cynthia Enloe
analyses the relationship between gender and militarism and describes 'the cultural groundwork for waging war':

> Militarizing gender before the first shot is fired is necessary
> for governments preparing for war. Men have to be social-
> ized from boyhood to see their masculine identities tied to
> protecting women while tolerating violence. Women have to
> be prepared from girlhood to admire men in uniforms and to
> see themselves as bandaging the wounds inflicted by violence
> rather than wielding it. [15]

Violence and silence are intimately linked for men. The conventional masculine script requires men to 'give 'em hell' – aggression,
violence and daring are required masculine activities, but not reflec-
tion on them, or discussion of them. As a response to the trauma of
war, the inability to speak arouses justified sympathy, and *The Not
Dead* is a very powerful film, not least because Armitage has given
a voice in it to what individual veterans have often been unable, or

have refused to articulate. The film attempts to heal a wound which is elsewhere in Armitage's work the object of baffled attention – a male habit of destructiveness which is inexplicable and which men refuse even to attempt to explain. Describing his work on a film called *Songbirds*, in which he wrote songs based on the experiences of women prisoners in Downview Prison in Surrey, Armitage says that most of the women are victims:

> Like the woman who was sexually assaulted with a weight-lifting bar. Like the woman who was raped with a revolver. Like the woman whose husband gave her regular black eyes to remind her that she belonged to him. Lurking in the background of each of these stories is a violent partner, a monstrous father, a desperate junkie, a heartless dealer, a sleazy pimp . . . some bastard, always a man. (*Gig*, p.54)

Male violence is a recurrent theme in Armitage's work, especially in his earliest writing where it is related to his experience of the probation service, and he comments on the response to it of 'a thick skin or a pair of tight lips' (*All Points North*, p. 8). 'Gooseberry Season' (*Kid*, pp1–2) and 'Hitcher' (*Book of Matches*, pp.46–7) both deal with close-mouthed murderers who feel no remorse, who feel in fact nothing at all, about the killings they have carried out. 'Poem' (*Kid*, p.29) is itself close-mouthed in its refusal to interpret the behaviour of a man recently dead, or even elaborate on a deadpan list of actions he carried out, including how he once punched his wife in the face, which is included alongside other actions, as though each is the equivalent of the other. What the actions have in common is that they are all domestic, and most of them are interactions with female members of his family – his daughter, his wife and his mother (no male family members are mentioned). It is implied, then, that the response to him at the end is also a female response and indicates that they still find his motives impossible to understand. And Sean O'Brien is right when he points out how even Armitage's garrulity can be close-mouthed, because the torrent of colloquial phrases and clichés for which he is famous resemble those long speeches in the plays of Harold Pinter where an abundance of speech is about a refusal to speak directly, and are about emotional avoidance (too little has been said about the gender aspects of this in Pinter). So even Armitage's garrulity is an expression of a masculine sensibility which refuses to communicate powerful feelings – as Peter Middleton says:

> Relationships need emotional labour, yet men have apparently been trained not to express emotion. Men are largely absent from the lives of young children, who therefore grow up emotionally supported by women. Because boys learn to separate from their mothers without finding a father ready to pass on emotional skills, unlike their sisters, they are not given much opportunity to learn them. Men's absence, and inexperience, perpetuate the situation, so that boys grow up unable to provide intramasculine emotional support (except perhaps in sport and war, which therefore become particularly attractive). [16]

That Armitage's own emotional responses are entirely different from this is abundantly clear not just from his life writing but from his love poems – 'To his Lost Lover' (*Book of Matches*, pp.51–4), for example, is as good as anything of this genre in contemporary poetry. But he is exceptionally adept at evoking the opposite, the shocking vacancy where masculine feeling ought to be and where it is deflected into compensatory fantasy or obsession. Armitage's second novel *The White Stuff* is preoccupied with this theme. Its central male character, Felix, is a social worker, so he is, in his own way, nurturing, and he is also intelligent and sensitive enough to suffer badly in sympathy with his wife Abbie about her inability to conceive, and her lack of family support other than himself, and her consequent need to track down her birth mother. And he is vulnerable enough to worry that when, near the end of the novel, she discovers a family she feels she can be a part of, that he will be excluded and alone. But he is not adept at explaining these feelings, even to his wife, and his shortcomings are continually discussed: he has never heard of 'multitasking' but once the concept is explained to him, and the view that men are less skilled at it than women, he has to agree that he struggles in contexts where it is required – that he struggles to load the dishwasher when the radio is on, that he once nicked his ear while shaving when the phone rang. He can daydream and drive, but driving and talking, even to his wife, is difficult for him: 'he'd often think of things he should've said, little phrases he could've used instead of what actually came out of his mouth.' (p. 134) Armitage derives much of the comic energy of his two novels from moments of often outrageous, specifically masculine, disaster or inadequacy. The most memorable scene in *The White Stuff* is when Felix, unable to get the erection required to produce sperm for the intra-uterine insemination his wife is supposed to receive at the local hospital, goes to his neighbour and closest friend Jed, to ask for his help. Baffled by what Felix wants, Jed, appalled, says 'You want me to . . . toss you off?' (p.148) But what Felix actually wants is for Jed to provide the required sperm.

While Felix's failings are treated with comic sympathy, other men in the novel, and men in general, are regarded with dismissive ruefulness. Abbie conducts vox pop surveys for a magazine article entitled 'What do men want?' Approaching one man and asking this question he gives the simple two-word reply 'Blow jobs' (p. 77). Early in the novel there is a short chapter describing a barbecue: here the subject of the final paragraphs is the contrasting behaviour of men and women. The men disperse, but the women 'consolidate their position in the heart of the garden and they communicate'. They discuss a range of subjects which include issues surrounding children and local schools, celebrities, 'the European Union and the Middle East and breast-feeding.' By contrast the men have scattered:

The male diaspora extends as far as the road, where one man is checking his brake pads and has placed a bottle of Budweiser precariously on the wing mirror of the car. It also includes one man watching an international rugby fixture on a portable telly in the children's playroom, and a man in the kitchen loading the dishwasher for the second time, and a man asleep under the cherry tree, and a man on his mobile phone by the gate, and a man rehearsing the military-style execution of a garden gnome with a water pistol to the back of its head, and a man under a pile of children on the trampoline, and a man whose bleeper went off ten minutes after he'd arrived and hasn't been seen since. (p. 55)

At the end of that chapter, 'the men come together to shake hands and seek out a task' (p. 55) – and the idea that it is in the focused activity of a task involving no human interaction that men are happiest is also the subject of 'The White Liners', which is about the tunnel-vision of men painting the white lines on all the varieties of roads. The poem compares them to drug addicts who extend their stash by adding 'crud' to it, and, like the men at the barbecue in *The White Stuff*, they have no tales to tell, being too much of a 'one-track mind' which simply does what it does, which in their case is more and more white lines. Armitage gets his characteristically rueful humour from the repetition of 'white lines' in that poem, and it is worth ending by stressing that note – that the comic mode is characteristic for him, and not just in the sense of wanting to be funny, but in the sense of having a world view which is best expressed through comedy with its generic emphasis on down-to-earth fun, on reconciliation and happy endings. So the slightly portentous note which Armitage strikes in 'Not the Furniture Game' (*Kid*, pp.66–8), which I discuss in 'Armitage's Contexts', is an exception which proves the rule because it is a parody of Ted Hughes's *Crow*, and derives its queasy disquiet from the gender attitudes in that poem, and still manages to derive humour out of its portentousness, alongside the disquiet, by poking respectful fun at Armitage's hero. It is worth comparing with 'You're Beautiful' (*Tyrannosaurus Rex*, pp.17–20) where the anxiety has disappeared and is replaced by a buoyant contrast of traditional gender characteristics in which the feminine is regarded as beautiful and the masculine as ugly. There is once again a parodic aspect but here of a work of much less daunting intellectual calibre – the book, published in 1992, by John Gray, *Men are from Mars, Women are from Venus*. As always with Armitage, though, the poem uses humour to make substantial points; the male speaker is voicing genuine regret about his masculine shortcomings, his tendency towards gratuitous aggression and boorishness, his dismissively rationalist attitutudes. But comedy, in Armitage's hands, is a substantial genre, and it is characteristic of him also to be involved in the comic mode when the aim is not even for laughs: 'After the Hurricane' returns to the greenhouse which provided that early image for the relationship between the poet and his father (*Zoom!*, p.13), and replaces the 'following in the father's footsteps' disposition with their sitting side by side as equals, next to the greenhouse, which has been damaged by high wind, drinking and smoking, and not even bothering to repair it.

Notes

1. Seamus Heaney, *Preoccupations: Selected Prose* 1968–78 (London: Faber, 1980) pp. 19, 143.

2. Ian Gregson, *The Male Image: Representations of Masculinity in Postwar Poetry* (Basingstoke: Macmillan, 1999).

3. Peter Sansom, 'Reading for Writing: Simon Armitage' in Lesley Jeffries and Peter Sansom, eds., *Contemporary Poems: Some Critical Approaches* (Huddersfield: Smith/Doorstop Books, 2000) p.79.

4. Judith Butler, *Gender Trouble* (London: Routledge, 1990) p. 59.

5. James Wood, 'Ever So Comfy', *London Review of Books*, 24th March 1994, p.23.

6. Luce Irigaray, *Speculum of the Other Woman* (Ithaca, New York: Cornell University Press, 1985) p. 185.

7. Simon Armitage, 'Simon Armitage' in Clare Brown and Don Paterson eds., *Don't Ask me What I Mean: Poets in their Own Words* (Basingstoke: Macmillan, 2003) pp.5–6.

8. David T. Evans, *Sexual Citizenship: the Material Construction of Sexualities* (New York: Routledge, 1993) p. 48.

9. Keith Sagar, 'Fourfold Vision in Ted Hughes' in Keith Sagar, ed. *The Achievement of Ted Hughes* p. 299.

10. Ted Hughes, *Lupercal* (London: Faber, 1960) p. 52.

11. Lynne Segal, *Slow Motion: Changing Masculinities, Changing Men* (London: Virago, 1990) p.102.

12. Sarah Broom, *Contemporary British and Irish Poetry* (Basingstoke: Macmillan, 2006)p.77.

13. Dennis O'Driscoll, 'Dome Laureate', *London Review of Books*, 27th April 2000, p. 40.

14. Sean O'Brien, *The Deregulated Muse* (Newcastle Upon Tyne: Bloodaxe, 1998) p.244.

15. Cynthia Enloe, *The Morning After: Sexual Politics at the End of the Cold War* (Berkeley and Los Angeles: University of California Press, 1993) p.63.

16. Peter Middleton, *The Inward Gaze: Masculinity and Subjectivity in Modern Culture* (London: Routledge, 1992) p.190.

4

ARMITAGE'S CHANGES OF PLACE

IN *GIG*, DESCRIBING a reading tour of the USA in November 2005, Armitage explains an anxiety he feels when performing outside Britain, about how the poems will 'translate'. The problem is not linguistic when the audience is American, but geographical:

> many of the poems are based in one particular village, looking out of one particular window, and at the time they were written had no ambitions beyond the visible horizon. Will the Yorkshire Moors and the motorway between Leeds and Manchester hold much meaning or interest for an audience in the American South? (p. 104)

His reading starts with 'The Shout' which he says has become a sort of 'signature tune' because it encapsulates so much of his own personal style. Armitage's account of the poem's background is therefore especially telling because he regards it as having a representative significance. He describes its narrative background, which I have already discussed in my chapter on 'Armitage's Voices'. What concerns me here is the closeness of the links between the poem and Armitage's native origins:

> There's one small geographical reference in the poem that will be meaningless to all but a few and is worth a quick mention.

Most of the houses in the village of Marsden are down in the bottom of a natural geographical bowl, with one notable exception. Fretwell's Farm sits on top of Binn Moor, way above every other dwelling. The apex of the roof and the chimney pot are just about visible from the picture window of my mum and dad's front room. And at night, so is the light in the farmyard. The Fretwells don't live there any more – in fact the true name of the farmstead is Acre Head. But when I was a boy, and it got dark, and the black of the night sky and the black of the moor merged into one unbroken backcloth of darkness, that light used to shine like a star, and people talked about Fretwell's farm as if it were a constellation – something you could steer a course by if you were lost and heading for home. (p. 106)

I have quoted that passage at length because it evokes so vividly a key aspect of Armitage's sensibility, his very concrete and particular sense of place, which is felt by readers of his poems as a constant presence, the sense that a high proportion of his writing has a very specific setting with its own parameters. It is an abiding specificity and by his own account here it has its source in his native origins, and it reveals as mistaken one major part of his personal image, especially his early image, as a 'whizzkid', because it reveals that a crucial part of his sensibility is retro in its adherence to the place where he was born and grew up. A major component of the postmodern is a geographical restlessness involving the idea, for example, that economies have changed so that they require mobile workforces, no-one has a job for life, and everyone must be prepared to shift regularly to seek work. The idea of stable, small communities, in which everyone knows everyone else and where most people spend their whole lives, is supposed to be a thing of the past. Certainly the theorising of Fredric Jameson, especially in his book *Postmodernism, Or, The Cultural Condition of Late Capitalism*, presents a picture in which everything has become thoroughly postmodern and no vestiges of the pre-postmodern still linger to complicate that picture.

Yet Armitage is a thoroughly contemporary writer whose adherence
to a single, native place plays a key role in his work.

For Armitage the specificities of place are linked to other characteristic specificities which are a major part of his power. On the first
page of Armitage's first novel *The Little Green Man*, the first-person
narrator, Barney, goes to look for the eponymous statuette in his
attic; he stands first at the top of the stairs, in the darkness but con-
scious of the light behind bedroom doors, and sunlight in the bath-
room which has passed through the frosted glass and reflects off
'chrome, mirrors and glass'. He pulls down the stepladders and feels
their cold in his hands, then climbs up:

> The blackness is dazzling, as if I've stuck my head through the
> roof into outer space. I reach for the light cord, somewhere to
> the left. A low-energy bulb brightens softly and slowly like an
> old valve, and the attic falls into place. Thick cobwebs flutter
> in a breeze that funnels up from the eaves. My breath steams
> in front of my face.
>
> I haul myself up, treading carefully over the joists, think-
> ing of the time my father's leg came bursting through the
> ceiling, as if God in heaven had taken the wrong step, expos-
> ing a skinny, white limb to the world below . . . Some of the
> slates have slipped or cracked. It's hard to believe that the
> outside is just inches away, that these thin sheets of stone
> tacked on to flimsy, wooden spars can keep out the sky. (p.1)

Attic poems are common in contemporary poetry, and they contain
the sort of objects I have left out and replaced with ellipsis – objects
such as suitcases and boxes full of books and magazines. The attic is
an obvious image for memory, and Armitage is too smart to bother
writing such an obvious poem. But in this opening to his novel he
brilliantly evokes the sense of a real attic, and he does so through
his ability simultaneously to locate and to name. At each stage of his
movements into the attic, Barney's position is pinpointed as though
with domestic map references, so that the reader knows exactly

where he is in relation to the first-floor rooms, the floor of the attic, and the roof, and that mapping is aided by the named features – the eaves, the joists, and the slates on their wooden spars.

A similar habit of mapping and naming is a feature of Armitage's poems. Part of its function is to produce a 'reality effect' which resembles the effect of realist notation in novels, where the point of what is being notated – ambient objects: the furniture in a room, for example – is that they have no representative or symbolic significance, they are what they are and therefore seem more 'real' because they are unliterary. So the post-coital couple in 'Missed It by that Much' (*Zoom!* p. 31) point out 'the landmarks down beneath us; me stood, you leant against the trig-point.' In 'Greenhouse' (*Zoom!*, p.13) when the young Armitage watches from his bedroom as his father enters their garden in the dark, he measures his distance away firstly from the sound of the 'hasp', (marking the moment when his father opens the gate), and then by the 'sparkle/ of a cufflink'. And Armitage's career starts – in the sense that they are the first lines in his first book – with his characterising of the victim of a blizzard in terms of the places in his life:

Heard the one about the guy from Heaton Mersey?
Wife at home, lover in Hyde, mistress
in Newton-le-Willows, and two pretty girls
in the top grade at Werneth prep.

Closer examination of those names reveals some possible symbolic meaning – Hyde suggesting, by contrast with home, the clandestine, (maybe even Jekyll and Hyde), and Newton-le-Willows suggesting that extra-marital affairs are exotically French. (Hints of punning trickery are often a shadowy feature in Armitage's poems: here, for example, it may be significant that 'VOLVO printed backwards in his frozen brow' would read 'OVLOV'.) Mostly, however, those names define the victim by locating him in a grid of places in the Manchester area; applying that grid and then adding to it a further map reference from *All Points North* to the M62 in mid-winter, that motorway 'like a belt drawn tightly across the waistline of Britain, with the buckle somewhere near Leeds' (p. 16), it would be possible to locate, with some exactness, the spot where the Volvo driver died.

For these reasons it is valid to talk about Armitage as a regional poet, however old-fashioned that concept may have become. Like Wordsworth and Hardy in England, and like William Carlos Williams, Robert Frost and Mary Oliver in the United States, Armitage can be discussed in terms of the abiding stabilities, the history, culture and geography of a place in which he has mostly lived and consistently returned to. The regional poet has distinct advantages in creating a sense of his, or her, own world, with its own integrity and its own highly recognisable landmarks. In his 'Introduction' to *Sir Gawain and the Green Knight*, Armitage talks about his motives for translating the medieval text being partly to do with his feelings of affinity with the anonymous northerner who wrote it, and detecting 'an echo of his own speech within the original' which includes words like 'bide', 'nobut', 'layke' and 'brid', which 'are still in usage in these parts, though mainly (and sadly) among members of the older generation' (p. vii).

A more recent prototype as northern poet is Samuel Laycock who was born, like Armitage, in Marsden, and wrote in Pennine dialect:

> There's only room for one poet in a village the size of Marsden, which makes Laycock somebody to move past or knock over. The best way to get at him is to take his poems and translate them from whatever version of English he wrote in to whatever version of English you practise yourself.

And Armitage has done precisely this: in 'To Poverty' (*Book of Matches*, pp. 38–9) and 'The Two of Us' (*The Dead Sea Poems*, pp. 32–4) where the theme of doubles is partly to do with the doubling of the contemporary poet with his nineteenth-century predecessor. So, on the first page of *All Points North*, Armitage says 'I know this place like the back of my hand . . . I know about belonging, and which of the people are my lot – us.' An important part of his achievement as a poet has been to invent a voice that is thoroughly associated with this place; as Denis O'Driscoll has written:

> In a 60th birthday tribute to Tony Harrison, Armitage noted that he had managed to find 'a written version of his voice, a sort of acceptable presentation of West Yorkshire utterance that stops short of dialect poetry.' Armitage's collections capture his own sprightly speech. Determined never to sound cloth-eared, he aerates his demotic language with emphatic rhythms and catchy rhymes (often half or para-rhymes), while also making sure that he sticks to the conventions of contemporary Yorkshire lingo. [1]

All Points North is an extended exercise in life writing focused on an attempt to define identity in relation to place, and includes a continual meditation on a Northerness which reaches beyond Yorkshire not just into Lancashire but also Northumberland, Humberside and Cumbria. The more Armitage stretches the exploration the more problematic the feeling of belonging becomes, and starts to unsettle the definition of identity that accompanies the feeling of belonging. It is at this point that the stabilities of place get compromised and it becomes evident that they cannot be relied upon once they are extended beyond the 'visible horizon' which Armitage defines in relation to 'The Shout', where the stability also refers to Armitage's boyhood but then undermines it with its horror at what has happened to the other boy, which involves his very radical shift of landscape to the other side of the world. Increasingly in Armitage's writing there is a preoccupation with the sense that place cannot be relied upon, a preoccupation with the different kinds of change which can afflict it.

To understand this thoroughly it is necessary to look at what happened to the perception of place in the twentieth century, and the best way to do that is to look at the writings of W.H. Auden, who is not only the poet who is most preoccupied with changes in the perception of place, and the poet who most effectively evokes them, but also a major influence on Simon Armitage. As I pointed out in 'Armitage's Contexts', Auden invented a personal landscape which he associated with a lost Eden, a mythical place immune to change, and which therefore does not share that human condition which is to be constantly in a state of becoming, constantly in transition. 'In Transit', by contrast, sites the poet jetlagged in an airport, in that 'nowhere' between places – admiring a hill he is not allowed to climb – and also between times, the 'frontier dividing/ Past from future'. [2] Armitage shares Auden's personal landscape but not the accompanying nostalgia, which is evident, for example, in the opening lines of Auden's 'Detective Story' (pp.151–2), which appear to be asking a rhetorical question which assumes that everyone carries around with them a personal setting that resembles Auden's. The certainties of place are compared to the certainties of genre: everyone must surely define themselves in relation to a 'home', a 'centre', just as detective stories define themselves by harping on familiar conventions of character and plot. When Auden's private world first appears in his published work, in 'The Watershed' (pp. 32–3), it represents exclusion rather than belonging. Its specificity and history contrast with the uncertain identity of the person 'Who stands' and 'sees' the derelict mine and tramlines. A watershed is literally a place but metaphorically a time of transition – the overlapping of those two meanings adumbrates Auden's habit of making landscape mark the boundary between being and becoming. 'The Watershed' starts, not with a description of the landscape, but by attempting to locate the point of view of a visitor whose understanding of what he sees is necessarily limited. That limitation is defined by its confinement to surface appearance, fragmentary glimpses, in comparison to the depth of the history recounted in the second and the long third sentences with their reference to graves and their mining imagery of shafts, workings and 'abandoned levels'. The contrast between surface and depth implies inauthenticity and leads to the naming of the visitor as a 'stranger' with whom the place 'will not communicate', and whose association with 'there' rather than 'here' makes him 'Aimless'.

The feeling of loss inflicted by the persistent memory of a personal landscape implies that landscape is always troubled by the threat and actuality of change which may affect the place itself or its inhabitants, or both. 'No Change of Place' (pp.33–4) is an early sign of Auden's awareness of those complexities, and associates the threat of change with the compressions of geographical space achieved by modern technologies such as the railway, the postal service and the telephone – however much a place may resemble its former self, these technologies have altered it by involving it more nearly with other places. The stranger in 'The Watershed' is also associated with technological change because the beams of his headlights cross a bedroom wall but fail to wake the locals from whom he is excluded, they slide across a surface and make no deep impression. 'No Change of Place', however, imagines a village where modern communications have been stricken by modernist fragmentation and failure to connect – the railway signals fail to work, the flowers that arrive by post are 'smashed' and the telephone conversations are 'stammered'. These failures of the modern create a place whose isolation – which would otherwise be impossible – continues, though it is both feared and desired, a dream that turns into a nightmare. It has reverted unreally, and inconsistently, to a pre-capitalist haven, which, when it is visited by a professional traveller, makes him 'dumb', and which remains untouched by 'brilliant capital'. That phrase refers both to money and to London and reinterprets the phrase 'no change', finding a reference to money in the title of the poem which thereby is made to refer to the way that places, as much as people, have become enmeshed in systems of exchange. There is a related pun on 'stock' in 'The Watershed' implying the inheritance of capital and indicating that the stranger is excluded as much for class as for geographical reasons. The paralysis that grips the community in 'No Change of Place' is imposed by anachronistic forces dominated by land, rather than capital, and personified by the 'gaitered gamekeeper' who patrols its boundary and prevents its youth absconding to that louche metropolis which, in 'The Capital', beckons nightly to the children of farmers.

'The Watershed' and 'No Change of Place' represent contrary states, of too much change and too little. In the former the loss of the personal setting leads to superficiality and restlessness, in the latter the personal setting has taken such a constricting hold that it stifles and inhibits development, but in both the interrogative 'Who' at the start indicates Auden's preoccupation with the interaction between place and identity. Elsewhere in Auden's work, however, the innocence of a place may be damaged simply by the passage of time: space and time as a binary pair are crucial in Auden's thought. They are combined in the ambiguity in the word 'watershed', and Auden considers that the detective story resembles the Quest for the Grail in using both 'maps (the ritual of space) and timetables (the ritual of time)' (p.151).

The undercover agent, or spy, is famously a key figure in early Auden. He sees the landscape from below, and that vision contrasts with that of the hawk, or airman, whose perspective from above has been more often discussed. Both points of view discover hidden truths about what they observe; unlike the superficiality of the outsider's understanding in 'The Watershed', these perspectives from below and above are given privileged access to truth by standing 'without'. The airman's vision is especially focused on a modernist perception of place because it introduces a montage in which the interconnectedness of places is displayed. The first line of 'Consider' (pp.61–2), 'Consider this and in our time', makes 'in our time' the premise of interpretation for what the hawk and the airman see below them but precedes it with 'and' as though it might also be possible to see what it was like before; the first lines of the second verse paragraph realize that possibility with a description of what happened 'Long ago'. The poem repeats the modernist habit of comparing the present with the past – as in *The Waste Land* where the comparison is made largely by ironic textual references – and its opening two lines imply that the vision from above is a peculiar characteristic of the modern condition. They indicate that 'Consider' is about the impact of time upon place, of 'our time' with its aeroplanes and radios which can draw places confusingly together, so that the reader is invited to join the people in the Sport Hotel where a band is playing which will be broadcast to others in a bewilderingly different location -'farmers and their dogs/ Sitting in kitchens in the stormy fens.' The differences in the two settings are not transcended through the broadcast link, but emphasized, and this verse paragraph has already insisted on division and conflict by making a 'border' the first landscape feature which is noticed, and describing the hotel's patrons in war-like imagery, as 'insufficient units' (a group but not sufficiently coherent to be unified), 'Dangerous, easy, in furs, in uniform'.

Disorientation is the carefully calculated effect of the first verse paragraph of 'Consider', and it culminates by spreading that geographical bewilderment into farmland in order to show that modern technologies have closed the gap between the city and the countryside, and inflict a sickness on the landscape, which suffers its symptoms more vividly than its inhabitants: harbours are silted, works are derelict, orchards are strangled. The sickness of these places has been inflicted by the contradictions of a capitalism whose apparent dynamism, whose novelty and unpredictability, leads to paralysis. Auden's imagery of place reflects those contradictions: the airman's speeding above and across leads to stasis.

When Armitage started to write, he entered a poetic context in which Auden's modernist scepticism about place had been absorbed: Auden was by far the most influential poet in postwar British poetry. This newly unstable sense of place was a radical departure in a poetic tradition which, especially since the Romantic movement, had been fascinated by landscape, and often taken a carefully notated location as its premise. Auden's influence must be joined to that of postwar cultural influences such as globalization and postcolonialism, which have sharpened a sense of how places which are geographically distant from each other can still interact and intermingle. So postmodern geographers such as Edward Soja and Doreen Massey have theorized about a radically altered sense of place which arises from these influences, and the technologies, such as television and the internet, associated with late capitalism. Doreen Massey describes 'the spatial' as constructed out of the multiplicity of social relations across all spatial scales, from the global reach of finance and telecommunications, through the geography of the tentacles of national political power, to the social relations within the town, the settlement, the household and the workplace. It is a way of thinking in terms of the ever-shifting geometry of social/power relations, and it forces into view the real multiplicities of space-time. [3]

The impact of these influences is especially striking in the case of Armitage because of his pronounced sense of place and space. In a writer with such a powerful feeling of belonging to his native village, who endows all his writing with such a precise spatial pinpointing, by providing such exact map references (of one sort or another) for his settings, the introduction of Audenesque effects of disorientation makes all the more impact. The title of his sonnet 'Look, Stranger' (*Kid*, p.35) refers to the first line of Auden's 'On this Island', in which the stranger resembles the character in 'The Watershed' as an estranged outsider, where estrangement can also be regarded as a literary technique, the defamiliarisation associated with the Russian formalist Viktor Shklovsky. Viewed from an unfamiliar angle, the island – in Auden's case, Britain – will be seen freshly, and as though for the first time. In Armitage's poem the island is more like Surtsey in that it has formed recently; Armitage has two poems on this subject in *Tyrannosaurus Rex versus the Corduroy Kid* (pp.34–5) and describes in *Gig* (pp.62–71) how the island was formed out of magma and ash from an underwater volcano. More importantly he talks in the prose work about its metaphorical meaning for him because the island was born in the same year that he was (1963) so that he identifies with it. These clues suggest that the island is a metaphor for personal development and identity, a theme it shares with the title poem of *Kid* and that volume's Robinson poems. In terms of place, then, Armitage may feel that his roots are in Marsden, but he also identifies with a bleak volcanic rock in the North Atlantic, and there is a strong feeling of disorientation in the opening line of 'Look, Stranger' where space and time are made each other's equivalents, as the 'century' is called a 'sea'. Further disorientation is caused by the shift in pronouns 'you', 'we', 'it', and by the uncertainty about whether the subject (who is 'skimmed' as in ducks and drakes) is a stone or a person, so that there may even be a reference to the concept, in Martin Heidegger, of 'thrownness'[4] which describes an existential bewilderment in which the self feels its presence in the world to have been torn out of context, feels that this presence is too starkly an unexplained fact. (Armitage could have found this idea, not just in Heidegger himself, but in Ted Hughes, whose thinking was influenced by Heidegger).

'Look Stranger' adopts a mode of riddling allegory which mounts towards a tentative personification, and this makes it one of Armitage's most difficult poems. Its difficulty hints at Armitage's struggle with its subject-matter, as he contends with the combined questions of identity and place. Its title suggests that its focus is partly on the question of poetic identity and is concerned with the same Oedipal conflict that preoccupies Robin in the title poem of *Kid* – that Armitage, in that battle for individuation which preoccupied Harold Bloom, is fighting to establish his own poetic selfhood in the face of the oppressive dominance of a powerful predecessor. Even in that process he is establishing his difference from Auden because the identity issue is one which preoccupied Auden, as a modernist poet, far less. Here the distinction made by Brian McHale[5] between the epistemological dominant of modernism, and the ontological dominant of postmodernism, is helpful, even if it is a generalization where exceptions can easily be noticed. Auden calls upon his stranger epistemologically in that his estranged knowledge (and ignorance) is invoked in order to freshen his poem's perspective in relation to an over-familiar subject, Britain (this island); to confirm McHale's point, as well, Auden is preoccupied with the detective story, which is the genre most concerned with epistemology. In Armitage, by contrast, the stranger also *is* the island, and the stranger is called upon ontologically to take an estranged look at himself, so that he seems to be concerned with that idea of a foreignness inside the self which I related to Julia Kristeva's book *Strangers to Ourselves* in my chapter on Armitage's Voices.[6]

Armitage is anxious about this issue even on the first page of *All Points North* when he is describing his sense of belonging. Despite that profound attachment to place, he declares that he lives 'on the border, between two states':

> We're a mixed bunch, although it's all relative, and one of us is no more mixed and no less relative than the rest. Me. On the other hand, sometimes it's somebody else. Those mixed-up days when it's easier to spot yourself in a crowd than recognize yourself in a mirror. On those occasions, it isn't me doing the rounds, getting about, going here, there and everywhere, but it isn't some stranger either. It's the other person, the second one. It's you. (p.1)

At the heart of home, Armitage is disoriented by a feeling of the unhomely, so that he seems very close to that concept of the 'heimlich' and the 'unheimlich' as it is defined by Freud in his essay 'The Uncanny': 'heimlich' in German means homely, but it also means 'secret' or 'concealed', and when these domestic secrets are revealed they produce a sense of the 'unheimlich' or uncanny. The most extensive discussion of the concept is by Nicholas Royle:

> The uncanny is ghostly. It is concerned with the strange, weird and mysterious, with a flickering sense (but not conviction) of something supernatural. The uncanny involves feelings of uncertainty, in particular regarding the reality of who one is and what is being experienced. Suddenly one's sense of oneself (of one's so-called 'personality' or 'sexuality', for example) seems strangely questionable. The uncanny is a crisis of the proper . . . a crisis of the natural, touching upon everything that one might have thought was 'part of nature': one's own nature, human nature, the nature of reality and the world . . . It can take the form of something familiar unexpectedly arising in a strange and unfamiliar context, or of something strange and unfamiliar unexpectedly arising in a familiar context. It can

consist in a sense of homeliness uprooted, the revelation of something unhomely at the heart of hearth and home.[7]

Kristeva refers to the sense of being strangers to ourselves as uncanny, because there the self is a home which is haunted by otherness. Similarly, for Armitage, the conviction that he lives on a border between two states extends far beyond the fact that Marsden is very close to the border with Lancashire. It even extends beyond the fact, which he does not mention, but which is important for his sensibility, that Marsden is on the border between the city and the countryside. Its significance for his work, especially in its treatment of place and identity, is in the idea of the liminal, or the interstitial, of the way that here is always on the border of elsewhere, so that in the title poem of *Zoom!* (p.80) the house quickly becomes the street, the town, the nation, the universe and then the galaxy. This also lies behind the shock at the end of 'The Shout' which is felt especially by readers who are aware of Armitage's sense of the precise locations in the poem as described in the passage from *Gig* which I quoted at the start of this chapter. What had previously been homely – two boys in their native landscape – has been uncannily disrupted by a suicide committed on the other side of the world, and the home has been invaded by that alien other place because the boy's shout reaches the poet even from that distance.

Armitage makes the invasion of one place by another the structural principle of *Killing Time* – the product of a commission by the New Millennium Experience Company where he was appointed as poet-in-residence by the Poetry Society. This is a thousand-line epic where, as the blurb puts it, 'a thousand years of history reaches its climax, with the last twelve months spooling past like newsreel'. More accurately, the blurb continues: 'In the Age of Communication, we find a world picked clean by microphone and camera, a world where nothing is sacred, secret or even true.' In fulfilling that remit, *Killing Time* imitates Louis MacNiece's *Autumn Journal* in its poetic structure, and also in its attempt at what Carol Rumens calls 'panoramic ambition',[8] which she thinks mostly fails because 'the form represents the dilution of his protean imagination rather than its reinforcement.' In arguing for this point, however, Rumens refers to one of the poem's features which is actually one of its strengths. 'The habit of beginning cantos with the news-bulletin link, "Meanwhile", for instance, disadvantages them from the outset. It seems an easy substitute for the art of splicing the end of one canto with the beginning of the next, an art MacNiece had at his fingertips.' (pp. 4–5) But this in fact hints that, while *Killing Time* is superficially MacNiecean, its more substantial influence is Auden, and the 'Meanwhile' structure indicates that it is evoking a simultaneity which is a key feature of Audenesque montage, in which distinctively different social groups and individuals, in geographically distant settings, are depicted performing a range of highly symptomatic actions. The microphone and the camera existed even in Auden's time and he is still the poet who has most extensively analysed their impact on the modern sensibility, not least in the radical altering of the perception of space and place. That perception is evoked in the poem's title in the extent to which, as well as referring to contemporary violence, and to the idling away of time, it suggests the foregrounding of spatial relationships. Armitage can therefore be seen, in *Killing Time*, as contributing to the Audenesque tradition of montage, and in one of the cantos describes two balloonists, Piccard and Jones, riding thermals across the equator, and being blessedly enabled to observe the world from above 'cartographically'(p.18) in a vision which vividly recalls the opening lines of Auden's 'Consider' with its airman and hawk seeing from above and therefore seeing connections unavailable to those below.

Elsewhere in Armitage's work, some of his most powerful moments arise from effects of disorientation produced by his colliding of one place with another so that they slide across each other tectonically. It is this idea which he draws upon when he wants, in 'The Convergence of the Twain' (*Travelling Songs*, pp. 21–2), to describe the carnage caused by the terrorist attack on the World Trade Centre. Alluding to Thomas Hardy's poem about the sinking of the Titanic, he imagines opposed forces which formed distantly from each other.

In Hardy's poem, the ship and the iceberg are similarly described as 'far and dissociate', and Armitage's focus on that idea can be related to Hardy's interest in what would come to be called montage – this aspect of his work has been regularly cited as an influence on that technique in the poems of W.H. Auden, notably in 'Consider'. So Armitage's poem is alluding to one from much earlier in what might be called a montage tradition, but the terms in which it does so reveal the contemporary poet's knowledge of theorizing about place which has been carried out since Hardy's time; 'The Convergence of the Twain' in its updated version refers to a contraction of space and time which causes the distant worlds to collide.

Similarly, in 'Revision Exercise with Textbook Examples' (*Kid*, pp.69–71) one of Armitage's school memories is used to provide a homely setting for imagining continental drift, and the Coriolis force, which call into large-scale question the inter-relationship between different parts of the world. That questioning leads to the invoking of a textbook example in which each house in a row which straddles the equator therefore experiences entirely different global phenomena. This early poem prefigures a key Armitage strategy in which defamiliarising is achieved by zooming and panning, by moving in very small and/or expanding out very wide from everyday experience in order to refresh it. Defamiliarising is such an important idea for Armitage's work that it is worth looking more closely at how Victor Shklovsky originally theorized it in his essay 'Art as Technique', [9] where he describes how perception becomes habitual and then 'automatic':

> Habitualization devours works, clothes, furniture, one's wife, and the fear of war ... And art exists that one may recover the sensation of life; it exists to make one feel things, to make the stone stony. The purpose of art is to impart the sensation of things as they are perceived and not as they are known. The technique of art is to make objects 'unfamiliar', to make forms difficult, to increase the difficulty and length of perception be-

cause the process of perception is an aesthetic end in itself and must be prolonged. (p.12)

The technique is especially important for Armitage because he deliberately focuses on familiar material. Michael Hulse[10] has been eloquent on this subject in defending Armitage against charges of being 'anecdotal': in fact the charge has been aimed at British poetry in general, and Hulse describes a Bulgarian dismissing it in these terms, which mean that it falls short 'of that ineffable otherness which is what true poetry is (of course) about'. Hulse makes his case by praising Armitage's 'For the Record' (*CloudCuckooLand*, pp 10–11), which describes the extraction of wisdom teeth: Hulse shows how it exemplifies Armitage's concern with 'stories of the lives people lead' because those are 'the place to look for human meanings', and he notices how the comparison, in the fourth stanza, of the extraction to an eviction, is 'an everyday thing, the stronger for being familiar, and strong too for being extended in dramatic form'. Hulse's point is that this is a key strength in Armitage, by contrast with 'poets who seem to value an image in proportion to its bizarreness'. It is this which makes defamiliarising so crucial for Armitage because his poems can make ordinary things seem bizarre – as the tongue does in 'For the Record' when it is compared to a 'mollusc'.

Armitage often achieves this effect through similes and metaphors such as those involving the mollusc and the eviction, which, as he puts it, 'bring about those moments of electrical comprehension that we get in literature, based on likeness or similitude or comparison' (*All Points North* p. 94), and which constitute for him a major part of the point of literature, of its reason for being. But I am focusing here on the effects of defamiliarising which, just as characteristically, he produces through his habit of putting places in dialogue with each other. The effect can be compared to the dialogue of points of view which I discuss in 'Armitage's Voices': just as Armitage makes voices overlap, he makes places interpenetrate each other, so that place itself, as a concept, is called into question, and – to adapt Shklovsky's point about the stone – he reveals the *placeness* of place. 'Revision Exercise' makes the school and the equator interact with each other; 'The Shout' similarly undermines the stability of Marsden with the realisation that it can be connected to Australia. The long sequence at the heart of *CloudCuckooLand* stretches places even further apart – much further – by placing Marsden in dialogue with the stars, because 'The Whole of the Sky' works like one of those modernist poems with a controlling metaphor that structures it around sets of comparison and contrast, and motifs that emerge as variants of imagery related to that core metaphor (T.S.Eliot's *The Waste Land*, for example, is structured around a metaphor that has its origins in fertility myths). Armitage's metaphor uses the shapes of different constellations as points of reference that attempt to structure human and earthly activities. He is knowledgeable about astronomy – it is another of those subjects, like geography and oceanography which, as I argue in 'Armitage's Contexts', distinguishes him from his predecessors and helps to shift the poetic paradigm from time to space, from depth to extended surface. So in *All Points North* one of his more esoteric attempts to define Northerness involves him in a TV program which includes an interview with Patrick Moore talking about the North Star (p.213). That book ends with an account of a church service in Marsden at Christmas, and the congregation stepping out under a night sky in which the constellations are clear and one of them points them out and names them, as Armitage's sequence does in the titles of individual poems: 'Aries', 'Orion', 'Taurus' and so on (p. 245). This person points a cigarette at those constellations to identify them, and then flicks it away

> Upwards into the bare branches of trees lining the graveyard,
> into the Milky Way. Then you split up, go your separate ways,
> towards different lives under the same patch of sky. (p. 246)

The title of the sequence suggests an attempt to see a 'bigger picture' that will make sense of the smaller, down-to-earth activities which it describes – which are mostly mundane, occasionally a bit odd in a way that is enjoyed, but also include the heroin addict who is stabbed in his backside (p.33), and the man who has his face slashed (p.109). The poem which describes that last incident includes the words 'motive' and 'meaning', because the police say the action lacked both, but those words loom especially large in a poem and hint that they represent an important moment thematically. And certainly the sequence seems as baffled as the police, and seems to use its core metaphor – as *The Waste Land* does – to proclaim the supreme difficulty of connecting anything with anything else, or even of shoring fragments against its ruins, and to be bewildered by the spectacle of such different lives being led 'under the same patch of sky'. It is this aspect of the poem which Sheenagh Pugh, reviewing it, focuses upon; referring to the Michael Hulse review that I have quoted, she quotes 'The Telescope' and says:

> Now this blankness, this *impossibility* of transcending the detail of our own lives and seeing beyond it into something more cosmic, supposing there is anything, may well be what Armitage's "quest" (Hulse, again) came up with, and what he wants to communicate. To this atheist reader, it sounds like a depressingly plausible world view. But for a poet, it also sounds like a dead end. [11]

But Pugh takes insufficient account of the rest of Armitage's work and so fails to see that 'The Whole of the Sky' is making a more specific point than one about meaninglessness – 'dead end', as a spatial metaphor, is precisely the opposite of the truth, which is to do with spaces which are enormously alive and extensive, which Armitage's subsequent work has continued to explore. Meaninglessness is merely the background against which he is establishing his specific theme about disorientation. The significance of the sequence is clearest in its opening poem 'The Mariner's Compass' (p. 25) for it is here that, defamiliarisingly and uncannily, vast spaces are made to infiltrate the home. Its speaker is simultaneously living in a rented house on his own, and single-handedly sailing a yatch around the world: his duvet covers resemble sails, and he finds flying fish next to his mail. Much of this turns on deliberate confusion over what is the tenor, and what the vehicle of the metaphor: is the refrigerator like a boat's engine, or the boat's engine like a refrigerator? Such uncanniness can be compared with that which appears in the play 'Eclipse', in the character of Lucy who represents placelessness because she lacks an origin, and mysteriously vanishes, and describes herself as a 'walking universe' who comes from wherever the best view of the planets is currently to be achieved (*CloudCuckooLand*, p. 142). That soliloquy provides a hint that Armitage's fascination with characters who vanish – which I discuss in 'Armitage's Voices' – should also be related to his problematising of place.

Another version of Armitagean disorientation comes from earlier in his career, in the title poem of *The Dead Sea Poems*, where the homely is surprisingly found in the exotic, as Armitage imagines discovering a manuscript of his own work in 'Qumran, where the Dead Sea Scrolls were unearthed in the 1940s'.[12] Elsewhere, the idea works the other way around – 'The Mariner's Compass' looks back to one of the sonnets in *Book of Matches* (p.11) and forward to 'An Expedition' (*The Universal Home Doctor*, pp. 24–6) as poems in which a radical disorientation is visited on a domestic interior by confusing it with bewilderingly extensive exotic terrain. In *Book of Matches* the speaker addresses his mother as they measure parts of the house; in the process, the walls become 'acres', the floors become 'prairies', traversing the bedrooms becomes a spacewalk, and the ending prefigures 'The Whole of the Sky', and even the opening of *Little Green Man*, in locating him in the attic where a window gives access to an 'endless sky'. The man and his mother working together hints at different gender attitudes to domestic space: 'An Expedition' pushes the idea further and makes the gendered component more explicit as it turns the home uncannily into a place where men can test their masculinity in those arenas where they have most wanted to express it – on frontiers, primitive stretches, sublimely inhospitable terrain. There is a similar idea about such territory invading the house in Auden's 'As I Walked Out One Evening', with its glacier and its desert entering a cupboard and a bed, but Armitage's gender preoccupation is his own and its presence in 'An Expedition' is made more evident by reference to a similar idea in his novel *The White Stuff* where he starts a chapter which focuses on the entirely different behaviour of the men and women at a barbecue with a paragraph about the contribution which the men make to the supplies:

> The men will take care of the very hot things and the very cold things. They'll deal with the extremes. They'll go to the Arctic Circle and to the Gates of Hell, but they won't be long. An hour and a half later they return with the smell of bacon on their hands, a trace of egg yolk between their teeth and a rolled newspaper in their back pockets. Sustenance and stimulation were required during their expedition. (p. 53)

'An Expedition' uses the same register, this time to refer, half-satirically, to DIY, and other male occupations in what is otherwise, in terms of traditional gendered geography, a female domain (Armitage in *Gig* (p.158) talks about his parents in precisely these terms, as dividing the house into ' "his and hers" '). So regions of the house are enormously expanded to become territories with names that evoke exotic and hazardous geology: 'Great Artex Shield', 'Plains of Anaglypta', 'Porcelain Rim', and these regions are negotiated in a register out of polar expeditions and the like, stressing masculine courage and endurance, the overcoming of terrible odds and meagre resources, in a refrain that reiterates pushing on regardless, reiterates dauntless penetration.

'Incredible', the last poem (p.66) in *The Universal Home Doctor* – a book whose title suggests a medicine for making the home universal, for uncannily infiltrating the home with the whole of the earth and sky – shares much in common with 'An Expedition' in its subversion of normal perceptions of domestic scale, of 'yardsticks'. But it adds other elements which show the link between concepts of place and concepts of ecology: these are linked, also, in the writings of ecocritics such as Lawrence Buell and Jonathan Bate. Ecological concern has been growing in Armitage's work for some time and looks clearly like a direction his work is going increasingly to take. In his 'Introduction' to his translation of *Sir Gawain and the Green Knight*, Armitage discusses the medieval poem in terms of its relevance now, finding it

> Oddly redolent of a more contemporary predicament, namely our complex and delicate relationship with the natural world. The *Gawain* poet had never heard of climate change and was not a prophet anticipating the onset of global warming. But medieval society lived hand in hand with nature, and nature was as much an enemy as a friend ... The knight who throws down the challenge at Camelot is both ghostly and real. Supernatural, yes, but also flesh and blood ... Gawain must negotiate a deal with a man who wears the colours of the leaves and the fields. He must strike an honest bargain with this manifestation of nature, and his future depends on it. (pp. vii-viii)

Part of Armitage's sensibility as a regional poet has always been his sense of how Marsden is set upon the margins of both the urban and the rural and his poems have repeatedly referred to the points at which the two interpenetrate each other. Being 'on the road' as a poet has been an important influence on his sense of place, and the interaction of places, and it has also raised his ecological awareness: *All Points North* describes a visit to the rainforest (pp. 113–6) which looks like the likely source of his poem 'The Wood for the Trees' (*The Universal Home Doctor*, pp. 30–1) and both accounts are lost in bewildered awe, with that Romantic sense of the sublime which involves fear as well as exhilaration, at the overpowering alienness of the experience. They also both manage to retain the Armitagean note of rueful comedy – as in the first line of the poem which declares unsurprise that, in the rainforest, it 'pissed down'. It is this note which offers the most promise for Armitage's future ecological writings, and which will distinguish him from other ecopoets: they will not be earnest, however serious they are, and his comic sensibility will insist on the earthy possibilities of regeneration, and the incongruous mingling of the ecological with the unsublimely human. There are some fine poems about birds towards the end of *Tyrannosaurus Rex*, but there is also 'Sloth' (p.42) which imagines that weird creature uncannily coming to rest in the attic above the poet's head, and locates him in terms of the vast perspective of the long slow time of the Big Bang and evolution, but also declares that the poet's wife would like to thrust a bomb up its backside.

A number of poems in *Seeing Stars* (2010) continue this trend. 'The Cuckoo' (pp.6–7) ends with its eponymous bird falling out of the sky and dying, but that has been preceded by a fabulatory account of the early life of James Cameron whose films include the first two *Terminator* films and *Avatar*, which establishes a setting in which cinema, and technology in general, suggest the predominance of simulacra. Accordingly the cuckoo turns out to be mechanical, and its combination of the artificial and the natural can be taken to represent Armitage's insistence on hybridity in these contexts – that nature must be respected and preserved but that must not lead to the pretence that humans can have access to it other than in combination with their own cultural constructions. That hybridity leads to incongruities and it is here that Armitage's characteristic comedy comes into play. The speaker of 'The Christening' (p.3) is a sperm whale who provides a range of information about himself in the register of natural history, except it is framed generically inside dramatic monologue, so that the register and the genre are at odds with each other and thereby mimic the impossibility, for humans, of transcending the boundaries of our species perspective. 'Beyond Huddersfield' (46–7) invents an especially memorable image that reflects Armitage's particular take on the ecological: the image is sadly comic, grotesquely disquieting. A recycling site contains, alongside the usual varieties of sorted rubbish, a skip which houses a black bear, with

> pizza toppings and chicken bones hanging from
> his matted coat, a red bandana knotted tightly around his
> skinny thigh, leaning to his work, busy at his groin, the
> gleaming needle digging for the sunken vein.

Notes

1. Dennis O'Driscoll, 'Dome Laureate', *London Review of Books,* 27th April 2000, p. 40.

2. W.H. Auden, *Collected Poems,* ed. Edward Mendelson (London: Faber, 1976) pp.539–40. All references to Auden's poems are to this volume.

3. Doreen Massey, *Space, Place and Gender* (Oxford: Blackwell, 1994) p. 4.

4. Martin Heidegger, *Being and Time* (Oxford: Blackwell, 1980) p.174.

5. Brian McHale, *Postmodernist Fiction* (London: Routledge, 1989) p.59.

6. Julia Kristeva, *Strangers to Ourselves,* trans. L.S.Roudiez, (London, Harvester Wheatsheaf, 1994) p.170.

7. Nicholas Royle, *The Uncanny* (Manchester University Press, 2003) p.1

8. Carol Rumens, *New Take on the Times: Simon Armitage's Poem for the Dome, Poetry Review* Spring 2000, p.4.

9. Victor Shklovsky, 'Art as Technique' in *Russian Formalist Criticism: Four Essays* trans. and ed. Lee T. Lemon and Marion J.Reis (Lincoln: University of Nebraska Press, 1965) pp.3–24.

10. Michael Hulse, 'Bright Boroughs of Heaven: Michael Hulse on Simon Armitage's "Cataloguing Hunger for Completeness" ', *Poetry Review* Autumn 1997, pp.66–7.

11. Sheenagh Pugh, 'Life, the Universe, and Everything', *Thumbscrew* Spring 1998, p. 37.

12. Simon Armitage, 'Simon Armitage' in Clare Brown and Don Paterson eds., *Don't Ask me What I Mean: Poets in their Own Words* (Basingstoke: Macmillan, 2003) p.4.

INDEX

Lightning Source UK Ltd.
Milton Keynes UK
UKHW010644120820
368106UK00003B/66